Vending Machine Success for Beginners

The Complete Guide to Starting a Vending Machine Business

Lena Voss

Warning

This book is intended to provide general information and guidance. The advice and strategies contained herein may not be suitable for every individual or business. The author and publisher are not liable for any damages or negative consequences from the use or application of the information presented in this book. Readers should consult with professionals, such as legal, financial, or business advisors, for specific recommendations tailored to their unique situations.

The author has made every effort to ensure the accuracy of the information within this book. However, due to the ever-changing nature of business, technology, and market conditions, the author cannot guarantee that the information provided is fully up-to-date or applicable to all circumstances.

TABLE OF CONTENT

INTRODUCTION:
The Day I Started My Vending Machine Journey

I've always been drawn to the thrill of building something from the ground up. Over the years, I've dabbled in everything from e-commerce to real estate, experiencing the highs of success and the lows of failure. But there's something uniquely satisfying about turning a simple concept into a profitable venture.

My vending machine journey began rather unexpectedly. It was August 2022, and I was sitting in a pediatrician's waiting room with my daughter. While she was occupied with her toys, my entrepreneurial mind wandered. I noticed a constant stream of people heading towards the vending machine. Every twenty seconds or so, someone was inserting coins and making a selection. There was even a short queue at one point.

I found myself counting the people who used the machine during my roughly 45-minute wait. Yes, you read that right. I counted 135 people. I know what you’re thinking: "This person must have been incredibly bored." You're not wrong! But there was something about that number that sparked a fire within me.

With more than one vending machine in the facility and more people coming and going (even before we arrived and after we left the facility), the potential was mind-blowing. I couldn’t shake the idea that there was a goldmine of opportunity in these seemingly ordinary machines. That day marked the beginning of my deep dive into the vending machine business.

Fast forward to today, and I’m proud to say I own and operate 50 vending machines and counting across Atlanta, with a team of dedicated staff in my employ. It’s been an exciting journey, and I’m eager to share the knowledge and experience I’ve gained with you.

Have you ever walked past a vending machine and thought, "I could do that"? Maybe you've even dreamed of owning your own vending machine business. Perhaps you've considered various passive income opportunities but haven't found the perfect fit. If so, you're not alone.

Most people are searching for ways to generate extra income without the traditional 9-to-5 grind. However, far fewer people see the potential for profit in the simple yet effective vending machine business.

This book is your guide to turning that dream into reality. Whether you're looking for a side hustle or a full-time business, vending machines can be a great way to make money. You don't need a lot of money to start, and you don't need any special skills.

What to Expect in This Book?

We'll start by giving you a clear picture of the industry, its perks, and the challenges you might face. Then, we'll shift focus to planning your business, from setting goals to crunching numbers.

Next, we'll help you understand your customers and find the perfect spots for your machines. Choosing the right vending machines is crucial, so we'll break down your options. Once you've nailed down your machines and locations, it's time to stock up on popular products and get those machines ready for business.

Keeping your machines running smoothly is key. We'll cover everything from regular maintenance to handling unexpected issues. To ensure your business stands out, we'll explore effective marketing strategies to attract customers and build a loyal following.

Managing your money is essential for any business. You'll learn how to set competitive prices, track your income and expenses, and stay on top of taxes. As your business grows, you might want to expand. We’ll show you how to do that without losing sight of what made you successful.

Maximizing profits is the ultimate goal. We'll teach you how to analyze your sales data to make smart decisions about your product mix. And to stay ahead of the curve, we'll explore the latest technology trends in the vending industry.

Great customer service is the backbone of any successful business. We'll show you how to keep your customers happy and coming back for more.

By the end of this book, you'll have a solid understanding of the vending machine business and the tools to build a profitable enterprise.

CHAPTER 1:
Understanding the Vending Machine Business

The vending machine industry is a dynamic and profitable sector experiencing consistent growth. Representing a substantial portion of the economy, the industry generates billions of dollars in annual revenue.

In fact, the National Automatic Merchandising Association (NAMA) represents the $34.9 billion US convenience services industry, of which vending is a significant component[i].

The global reach of this industry is impressive. According to Worldmetrics.org (2024), the global vending machine market size is expected to reach a staggering $87.5 billion by 2025. This growth is fueled by factors like increasing urbanization, rising disposable income, and the adoption of smart vending technologies[ii].

Here in the United States alone, the vending machine industry boasts over 7 million machines, providing convenient access to snacks, drinks, and other products across the country[iii]. This network not only satisfies consumer needs but also contributes significantly to the workforce. The vending industry supports approximately 1.5 million jobs in the U.S., highlighting its economic impact beyond direct sales[iv].

My business is a testament to this industry's job-creating potential. With over 50 dedicated individuals working together, we manage a fleet of vending machines across Atlanta. Our team's efforts contribute to the local economy by providing employment opportunities, generating tax revenue, and supporting other businesses in the supply chain.

Imagine the positive impact you can make on your community by starting your own thriving vending machine business. By creating jobs, generating revenue, and contributing to the local economy, you can become a catalyst for growth and development. Every vending machine you install has the potential to stimulate economic activity, from the purchase of products to the maintenance and repair services required to keep your machines running smoothly.

Technology is also transforming the vending machine landscape. According to Verifiedmarketresearch.com (2024), the global smart vending machine market is projected to grow at a rapid pace, with a Compound Annual Growth Rate (CAGR) of 10.69% from 2024 to 2030. These smart machines offer features like cashless payment options, digital displays, and real-time inventory management, enhancing both the customer experience and operational efficiency for business owners[v].

These statistics paint a clear picture: the vending machine industry is a thriving and growing business sector with a global reach and a significant impact on the economy.

Keep in mind that, beyond the traditional snacks and drinks, the industry has diversified to include a wide range of products. From fresh produce and electronics to pharmaceuticals, vending machines have become platforms for delivering diverse goods and services. This expansion has created new opportunities for entrepreneurs, allowing us to tap into niche markets and cater to specific consumer needs.

The Evolution of Vending Machines

Vending machines have undergone a remarkable transformation from simple coin-operated dispensers to sophisticated retail outlets. The integration of technology has revolutionized the industry, enhancing both consumer experience and operational efficiency.

Today's vending machines boast features like cashless payment options, digital displays, and advanced inventory management systems.

These innovations have transformed the way consumers interact with vending machines and provided business owners with valuable data insights.

My own business has embraced this technological evolution. With a fleet of approximately 22 smart vending machines, I've firsthand experienced the benefits of remote monitoring, real-time inventory tracking, and data-driven decision-making. By leveraging these technologies, I've been able to optimize product selections, prevent stockouts, and identify high-performing locations.

These advancements have not only improved my operational efficiency but have also elevated the overall customer experience. Customers appreciate the convenience of cashless payments and the ability to see product options clearly displayed on the machine.

Benefits of the Vending Machine Business

One of the most appealing aspects of owning a vending machine business is the *potential for passive income*. Imagine waking up to consistent earnings generated by machines operating around the clock. That's the beauty of this venture. While there's initial setup and management involved, the long-term rewards can be substantial. For instance, during busy months, my vending machines have generated enough to cover several of my personal expenses, giving me a sense of financial freedom.

Another advantage is the *low barrier to entry*. Unlike many businesses that require significant upfront capital, you can start a vending machine business with a relatively modest investment. This makes it an attractive option for entrepreneurs with limited funds. When I first started, I invested a portion of my savings and gradually expanded my operation as profits increased.

The *flexibility* of a vending machine business is a game-changer. You can structure it to fit your lifestyle. Whether you're looking for a full-time income or a supplemental source of revenue, this business model can accommodate your goals. For me, it started as an experimental side hustle, and as it grew, I was able to dedicate more time to it.

Diversifying your income streams is crucial for financial stability. A vending machine business allows you to explore various product offerings and locations. By carefully selecting products and machine placements, you can create multiple revenue streams. For example, I've experimented with different product mixes in various locations to identify what sells best. This approach has helped me mitigate risks and ensure a steady income.

Imagine the freedom of owning a business that generates income while you focus on other passions or spend quality time with loved ones. A vending machine business can offer you that.

Challenges of the Vending Machine Business

While the vending machine business offers immense potential, it's essential to acknowledge the challenges that come with it. These hurdles, while initially daunting, can be overcome with experience, strategic planning, and adaptability.

Location, Location, Location: Finding the right spots for my vending machines was initially a trial-and-error process. I remember spending countless hours driving around Atlanta, looking for high-traffic areas with minimal competition. While some locations were instant hits, others underperformed. Over time, I've learned to analyze foot traffic patterns, demographics, and competitor activity to make more informed decisions. Now, I rely on data analytics and customer feedback to optimize my machine placement.

Inventory Management: Balancing product availability with minimizing waste is a constant juggle. In the early days, I often overstocked or understocked certain items, leading to lost sales or expired products. To address this, I implemented a detailed inventory tracking system and started analyzing sales data to predict demand. Now, I'm able to fine-tune my product assortment and order quantities based on historical sales patterns.

Maintenance and Repairs: Vending machines are like any other piece of equipment; they require regular maintenance. In the beginning, breakdowns were frequent and unexpected, causing significant disruptions. To mitigate this, I've built strong relationships with repair technicians and invested in preventive maintenance programs. Regular inspections and timely repairs have significantly reduced downtime and increased machine reliability.

Vandalism and Theft: Protecting my vending machines from vandalism and theft has been an ongoing concern. I've experienced everything from minor damage to complete machine theft. To deter vandalism, I've installed surveillance cameras and implemented security measures like reinforced casings. For theft prevention, I've explored options like cash management systems and GPS tracking. While challenges persist, these measures have helped to minimize losses.

Regulations and Permits: Navigating the complex web of regulations and permits can be overwhelming for anyone entering the vending machine business. Each city and state in the United States has its own set of rules, making it essential to understand the legal landscape before launching your operation.

In Atlanta, where my vending business is based, obtaining the necessary permits and licenses required careful planning and coordination with city officials. I had to comply with health and safety regulations, zoning laws, and business licensing requirements. The City of Atlanta's website, www.atlantaga.gov, is a valuable resource for obtaining information on business licenses and permits.

While the process can be time-consuming, it's crucial to ensure legal compliance and avoid potential penalties. For those operating outside of Atlanta or the United States, researching local laws and ordinances is the first step. Contacting your city's business development office or economic development department can provide valuable information. Additionally, trade associations related to the vending industry may offer resources and guidance on navigating regulatory requirements.

Most states and provinces have online portals where you can search for business licenses and permits. Example search queries: *"[State name] vending machine permit," "[Province name] business license for vending machine"*

Remember, compliance with local regulations is not just about avoiding penalties; it's about building trust with your community and ensuring a safe and enjoyable experience for your customers. By investing time and effort into understanding the legal framework, you can lay a solid foundation for your vending machine business.

While these challenges initially posed significant hurdles, I've learned to adapt and overcome them through experience and strategic planning. By understanding the potential obstacles and implementing effective solutions, you can build a successful vending machine business.

Understanding the vending machine industry is crucial for anyone looking to venture into this exciting business. By understanding the industry's potential, challenges, and the evolving technological landscape, you've taken the first step towards building a successful vending machine empire.

Up next: We will discuss the essential planning stages of your vending machine journey. From setting clear goals to crafting a detailed business plan and estimating startup costs, I'll equip you with the tools to lay a solid foundation for your venture.

CHAPTER 2:
Planning Your Vending Machine Business

Starting my vending machine journey was almost like a leap into the unknown. Armed with nothing more than a few online videos touting the profitability of the vending machine business, I decided to take the plunge.

Initially, I had a naive notion of a single vending machine manufacturer dominating the market. But after making countless calls to gather information, I quickly realized the industry was more diverse than I'd imagined.

With a modest investment, I purchased two used machines to kickstart my venture. The first was a Wittern FSI 3141 USI with a large glass front. This model, priced at $2950, offered 35 item selections and a capacity for 216 items. Its key features included a user-friendly interface, electronic pricing, and a pull-out tray for easy loading. It was a solid foundation for my business.

The second machine was a significant upgrade. I invested $3600 in a more advanced model boasting features like individual product pricing, detailed sales reports, and energy-saving settings. Its all-metal product trays and anti-theft design were additional perks. This machine, with its larger capacity and advanced technology, promised to elevate my vending operation.

Strategically, I placed one machine on a bustling college campus, targeting students with a penchant for late-night snacks. The other found its home in what was supposed to be a high-traffic office building, catering to busy professionals seeking quick refreshments.

These initial placements were a rollercoaster of emotions. The campus machine quickly became a cash cow, especially during exam periods. The office building machine, however, required more patience. It gradually picked up momentum, demonstrating the importance of location selection.

These early experiences were invaluable. They taught me the nuances of consumer behavior, machine performance, and the overall dynamics of the vending machine business.

Setting Your Goals

Before diving headfirst into the world of vending machines, it's crucial to define your goals. What do you hope to achieve with this venture? Are you aiming for a modest supplemental income, a full-time replacement, or building a vending empire? How much do you expect to earn from your machine(s)? Clearly defining your objectives will guide your decisions and keep you focused.

When I started, my goals were modest. Truthfully, given my involvement in real estate and internet marketing, I primarily viewed the vending machine business as a means to diversify my income streams and explore a new business model.

With two vending machines, I aimed to generate an extra $800 a month. I naively projected $400 in monthly revenue from each machine, based on anticipated profits, after deducting the initial capital invested in inventory. Reality, as it often does, had other plans. The campus machine exceeded expectations, generating nearly $600 in its first month. The energy of the students, coupled with a strategic product mix, proved to be a winning combination. The office building machine, however, struggled to gain traction, generating less than half of my projected earnings.

These early experiences served as a valuable reality check, reinforcing the importance of data-driven goal setting, a principle I've long upheld in my business ventures. The stark contrast between the campus machine's performance and the office machine's underachievement highlighted the need for a more granular approach.

My original goal of $800 monthly profit, divided equally between the two machines, proved overly ambitious at the time. Given its slower performance, I adjusted my expectations for the office machine to a more conservative $200 per month. This recalibration still resulted in a revised total monthly revenue projection of $800, a more accurate reflection of the business's early performance.

However, the difference between expectation and reality didn't just impact my financial projections—it had broader implications for my business mindset and operations. Setting unrealistic goals can create a ripple effect of challenges, both mentally and financially. For instance, when my office machine underperformed, I initially felt disappointed and stressed. I began questioning my choices, wondering if I had made a mistake in placing the machine there or if the product selection was wrong. This self-doubt was distracting and could have easily led me to make hasty decisions, like drastically changing the product mix without proper analysis, which would have only compounded the problem.

Financially, setting overly optimistic goals can put a strain on cash flow. Expecting a certain level of revenue, I initially stocked the office machine with more inventory than needed, which tied up capital in products that weren't moving as fast as anticipated. This meant that my money was sitting on the shelves, rather than being reinvested or used elsewhere in the business. If not managed carefully, this kind of overstocking can lead to waste, especially with items that have shorter shelf lives.

Unrealistic goals also affect the quality of operations. Trying to force higher sales to meet an overly ambitious target can lead to decisions that compromise the customer experience, such as stocking cheaper, lower-quality products in an effort to cut costs. This could damage the reputation of the machine and reduce customer trust, ultimately hurting long-term sales.

On a personal level, constantly missing your targets can be mentally exhausting. I remember feeling overwhelmed when the numbers didn't add up, and it affected my focus on other aspects of the business. The pressure to meet those initial targets often made me second-guess every decision, which is a tough place to be as an entrepreneur.

That's why you must set realistic, data-driven goals right from the start. It's not just about keeping your finances in check—it's also about protecting your mental well-being and the quality of your business. By adjusting my expectations to reflect real-world data, I found myself approaching my vending machine business with a clearer mind, better financial health, and a renewed commitment to providing the best products to my customers.

A Practical Approach to Goal Setting

Setting clear, achievable goals is essential for the success of your vending machine business. Drawing from my experience, I've found that a data-driven approach is invaluable.

Let's break down the process:

Identify your financial goals: Determine your desired monthly, quarterly, or annual income from your vending machines. For instance, if you're looking for a supplemental income, aim for a specific amount to add to your current earnings. Having a clear figure in mind, like aiming to earn $1,000 per month from your vending machines, sets a tangible target to work toward. Without a specific amount, your financial goals become vague, making it hard to measure success or failure. A common beginner mistake is setting broad goals like "earn more money," which lacks direction and clarity. When you define a precise figure, you can better plan your product selection, pricing strategy, and location placements, ultimately making your business more focused and efficient.

Conduct market research: Analyze your target market, competitor pricing, and average sales per machine in your area. For example, research the average revenue generated by vending machines in college campuses or office buildings. We will expand on conducting market research in the next chapter.

Set realistic expectations: Based on your research and initial machine performance, establish achievable revenue targets for each machine. Understandably, as a complete newbie to the business who doesn't have a past performance report to rely on, you can start by researching similar machines in your target locations. Look at factors that affect performance, such as foot traffic, product mix, pricing, and placement within the location. Adjust your expectations based on what's typical in the industry. For instance, if you find that vending machines in office buildings average $200 a month, start with a modest goal of $150 and work toward improving it. Performance can be influenced by factors like product selection, machine visibility, and promotional efforts. To improve, try testing different product mixes, adjusting prices, or enhancing your machine's visibility with better lighting or signage.

Create a timeline: Set short-term and long-term goals. For example, aim to achieve a specific revenue target within the first six months, then reassess and adjust your goals for the following year.

Review and adjust: Regularly analyze your performance and compare it to your goals. Make necessary adjustments to your targets based on market conditions, economic factors, and machine performance.

Remember, goals should be SMART: Specific, Measurable, Achievable, Relevant, and Time-bound. For example, instead of a vague goal like "increase profits," aim for "increase monthly revenue by 15% within the next quarter." Here's why this goal is SMART:

- **Specific:** The goal clearly states the target (increase revenue) and the percentage (15%).
- **Measurable:** You can track your sales data to see if the 15% increase is met.
- **Achievable:** A 15% increase is a reasonable target based on past performance and market research.
- **Relevant:** Increasing revenue directly impacts the overall success of your business.
- **Time-bound:** The goal sets a specific timeframe (within the next quarter) to achieve this.

Here's another example of a SMART goal: Instead of saying, "I need to add more machines to my fleet soon," set a goal like, "I will add 3 new machines to my fleet by the end of the year." So why is this SMART?

- **Specific:** The goal is clear—add three new vending machines.
- **Measurable:** You can count the machines added to track progress.
- **Achievable:** Consider your budget, available locations, and supplier relationships to ensure this goal is within reach.

- **Relevant:** Expanding your fleet directly contributes to your business growth and income potential.
- **Time-bound:** The deadline is set (by the end of the year), giving you a clear timeframe.

By following these steps and regularly evaluating your performance, you'll be well-equipped to achieve your vending machine business goals.

Creating a Business Plan

A well-structured business plan is your roadmap to success. It outlines your business concept, target market, financial projections, and operational strategies. While it might seem daunting, creating a business plan doesn't have to be complicated. When I started my vending machine business, I learned this lesson the hard way.

Initially, I was excited to dive in, and my business plan was more about getting things on paper than truly understanding the market. I was overly optimistic with my financial projections, setting revenue targets that were far from realistic. I expected to make profits almost immediately, which led me to overspend on high-end machines and inventory without fully grasping my break-even point. This misstep put a strain on my finances, and I found myself scrambling to make ends meet when sales didn't match my projections.

On the other hand, one part I did well was my clear definition of the business concept. I spent time identifying my target market—

college students in the Atlanta area who needed quick snack options between classes. My focus on providing healthier alternatives was a hit, which kept me going even when my financial projections didn't initially pan out.

The biggest takeaway for me was that a business plan isn't just a formality—it's a crucial guide that requires ongoing adjustments based on real-world data. My experience taught me that having a realistic approach to projections, a well-defined target market, and a solid sales strategy can make or break your business. Now, let's look at the key elements of a solid business plan.

Here's a basic outline to get you started:

Executive Summary

This concise overview should encapsulate your business concept, target market, and financial projections. For example:

This business plan outlines the strategy for a vending machine operation targeting [college campuses in the Atlanta metropolitan area]. By providing convenient access to snacks, beverages, and other products, we aim to generate a consistent revenue stream while catering to the needs of the [student population]. Initial projections indicate a monthly revenue of [$2,500] within the first year of operation.

Business Description

Clearly define your business concept, target market, and unique selling proposition.

Our business, [Your Business Name], will operate vending machines strategically placed on [college campuses within the Atlanta metropolitan area]. Our target market consists primarily of [college students] seeking convenient and affordable snack and beverage options. Our unique selling proposition lies in offering a curated selection of products, including healthy alternatives, and maintaining well-stocked, clean machines.

Market Analysis

Conduct thorough research on your target market and competitive landscape.

The [college student market in Atlanta] is a thriving demographic with a growing demand for convenient food and beverage options. Key competitors include existing vending machine operators on campus and campus cafeterias. By offering a diverse product selection and focusing on customer satisfaction, we aim to differentiate our business and capture a significant market share.

Organization and Management

Outline your business structure and management team.

Initially, the business will operate as a [sole proprietorship] under the name [Your Business Name]. As the [sole owner and operator], I will handle all aspects of the business, from machine placement and inventory management to maintenance and financial oversight.

However, as the business grows and expands, I anticipate the need for additional personnel. A potential organizational structure could involve hiring part-time employees or contractors to assist with machine restocking, maintenance, and customer service. The core management team would consist of myself as the owner and a general manager responsible for day-to-day operations.

By implementing a structured approach to management, I aim to ensure efficient operations and scalability as the business grows.

Service or Product Line

Detail the products you'll offer and your pricing strategy.

The vending machines will offer a variety of snacks, beverages, and potentially other products such as personal care items. Product selection will be based on market research and customer preferences. Pricing will be competitive with other vending machines in the area, with a focus on providing value for customers.

Marketing and Sales Strategy

Outline your marketing plan to attract customers and generate sales.

Marketing efforts will focus on building brand awareness and customer loyalty. Strategies include on-machine advertising, social media campaigns, and partnerships with campus organizations. Customer feedback will be actively sought to refine product offerings and improve customer satisfaction.

Financial Projections

Create income statements, balance sheets, and cash flow statements to forecast your business's financial performance.

Financial projections for the first year of operation indicate a total revenue of [$30,000], with estimated expenses of [$15,000], resulting in a net profit of $[15,000]. These projections are based on [specific assumptions, such as number of machines, average revenue per machine, and operating costs].

Remember to replace the placeholders with your specific information. This outline provides a solid foundation for your vending machine business plan. You can expand on each section as needed to provide more detailed information.

Remember, a business plan is a living document. It should be updated regularly to reflect changes in your business and the market.

Estimating Startup Costs and Potential Profits

Starting a vending machine business requires upfront investments. However, before we break down the potential costs, it's crucial to highlight some common beginner mistakes when making these estimations and how they can negatively impact your business:

Underestimating Initial Costs:

One of the most common mistakes is underestimating the full scope of initial costs, such as maintenance, transportation, or location fees.

Many new operators budget only for the machines and inventory, forgetting about the smaller, ongoing costs that add up over time. This oversight can lead to cash flow problems and limit your ability to reinvest in your business. To avoid this, ensure you include every potential expense, no matter how small.

Overestimating Sales Volumes and Revenue:

It's easy to assume that your vending machines will be busy all day, every day. Beginners often set high sales targets without considering factors like seasonal fluctuations, location-specific demand, or machine downtime. Overestimating sales can lead to unrealistic financial projections, causing you to invest more than necessary and possibly leading to financial strain when the actual sales don't meet expectations.

Ignoring Location-Specific Challenges:

Location is everything in the vending machine business, but not all high-traffic locations are created equal. A common mistake is assuming that every busy spot will guarantee high sales. Factors like competition, customer preferences, and location-specific regulations can affect performance. This mistake can result in underperforming machines and wasted investments.

Failing to Account for Operational Costs:

Many new vending machine owners overlook ongoing operational costs like electricity, maintenance, and inventory replenishment. Not accounting for these costs can severely impact your profit margins, turning what seems like a profitable venture on paper into a struggle to break even.

Lack of a Buffer for Unexpected Expenses: Unexpected costs such as repairs, replacement parts, or sudden changes in location fees can catch new operators off guard. Without a buffer, these unforeseen expenses can quickly eat into your profits, creating financial instability. Always set aside a contingency fund to cover these potential surprises.

By being mindful of these pitfalls, you can create a more accurate and reliable estimation of your startup costs and potential profits, setting a solid foundation for your vending machine business.

Now, let's dive into the detailed breakdown of the costs you should expect and how to estimate your profits effectively.

Vending machines: My initial investment included two machines priced at $2950 and $3600, respectively. Depending on size, features, and condition, expect to spend anywhere from a few hundred to several thousand dollars per machine.

Inventory: The initial stock of products will depend on the size of your machines and the variety of items you offer. A conservative estimate for initial inventory is around $500 to $1,000.

Location fees: Some locations may charge a fee for vending machine placement. To determine a competitive lease rate, research similar locations in your area. Contact other vending machine operators or property managers to gather information on going rates. Typically, lease agreements involve paying a percentage of your monthly revenue, often ranging from 15% to 20%. However, the specific rate can vary based on factors like location desirability, foot traffic, and the terms of the lease.

Permits and licenses: Depending on your location, you might need to obtain permits or licenses to operate vending machines. The costs for permits and licenses can range from $50 upwards, depending on local regulations. It's essential to research local regulations and budget accordingly.

Transportation: Allocate funds for a reliable vehicle or transportation services for machine delivery and restocking.

Miscellaneous expenses: This includes items like cleaning supplies, change, and marketing materials.

For my initial setup, I invested around $8,850 in two vending machines, including inventory, transportation, licenses, machine placement, etc. Here's what it looked like:

Expense Category	Details	Amount
Vending Machines	Machine 1	$2,950
	Machine 2	$3,600
	Total for machines	$6,550
Initial Inventory	$500 per machine x 2 machines	$1,000
Location Fees	20% of $800 monthly revenue	$160
Permits and Licenses	Government	$120
Transportation	Machine delivery	$150
Miscellaneous Expenses	Cleaning supplies, change, marketing	$300
Total Initial Setup Cost		**$8,280**

So, my initial setup cost for starting my business with two machines was $8,280.

Estimating Potential Profits

To accurately estimate potential profits, a thorough understanding of various factors is essential.

Machine location: High-traffic areas generally yield higher sales. Analyze foot traffic patterns in potential locations. We talk more on this in chapter five.

Product pricing: Conduct a competitive analysis of product prices in your area. Consider factors like consumer demand and profit margins when setting your prices.

Sales volume: Estimate average daily, weekly, or monthly sales based on similar vending machines in your target locations.

Operating costs: Factor in expenses such as product costs, machine maintenance, electricity, and location fees.

Market research is crucial for accurate estimations. Visit various locations with vending machines, observe customer behavior, and note popular products. You can also conduct informal surveys to gauge product preferences.

For example, if you estimate an average daily sale of 50 items per machine, with an average selling price of $2 per item, your daily revenue would be $100. Assuming 20 operating days per month, your monthly revenue per machine would be $2,000.

Remember: These are rough estimates. Actual profits will vary based on numerous factors, including location, product mix, pricing strategy, and operational efficiency. Continuous monitoring and adjustments are essential for maximizing profitability.

By carefully considering these factors, you can create a realistic financial projection for your vending machine business.

Up next: We will talk more about market research. The success of your venture hinges on understanding your target audience, analyzing competitors, and identifying prime locations for your vending machines.

CHAPTER 3:
Researching the Market

Knowing your target audience is fundamental to the success of any business, and the vending machine industry is no exception. To optimize your product offerings and location selection, it's essential to understand who your potential customers are and what they want.

For instance, when I initially launched my vending machine business near a college campus, I made the classic assumption that students would primarily crave sugary snacks. While there was some demand for these items, and I even exceeded my $400/month goal for that machine, I quickly realized that this wasn't the entire picture. There was potential for even more sales!

Sales data revealed an unexpected trend: students were showing a growing preference for healthier options. To understand this shift better, I started reading academic research papers related to student's diet and nutrition. Studies from reputable sources like the National Library of Medicine confirmed my observations.

Research published by Frontiers in Nutrition in 2021 highlighted a growing dissatisfaction among students with the typical vending machine fare[vi]. They expressed a strong desire for more nutritious options like fresh fruits, vegetables, and higher-protein snacks. Another study published by BMC Public Health back in 2015 confirmed this, highlighting the students' desire for healthier choices[vii].

This valuable insight led to a pivotal adjustment in my business strategy. By tailoring my product offerings to meet the evolving needs of my target audience, I was able to significantly increase sales and customer satisfaction.

In researching, as a complete beginner, you might wonder whether to choose a location first and then decide on the product mix, or to identify your target audience first and then find locations that cater to them. At least, the thought crossed my mind when I started. Both approaches have their merits:

- **Location First, Audience Second:** This approach works well if you already have access to a high-traffic spot, like an office building or gym. In this case, once you've secured the location, your next step would be to research the audience frequenting that spot and adjust your product offerings to meet their preferences.
- **Audience First, Location Second:** If you have a clear idea of your ideal customer—like college students seeking healthy snacks—start by identifying the audience first. From there, look for locations that align with this group, such as college campuses or student housing complexes. This ensures that your location and product offerings are in sync from the beginning.

Both methods are viable, and choosing the right approach depends on your starting point, whether it's access to a great location or a clear target audience.

However, the key takeaway here is the importance of staying informed about consumer trends and preferences. By understanding your customers' desires, you can position your vending machine business for long-term success.

Like I said, this research was a real turning point for my business. So, here's what I did:

Reduced the Sugary Snacks: Instead of completely eliminating popular items, I opted to reduce their presence and introduce even more healthier alternatives. So, in came a selection of granola bars, a trail mix with dried fruits and nuts, and bottled water.

Catered to Convenience: I knew portion control was important for students, so I offered healthy snacks in smaller, individually packaged options.

Spread the Word: I partnered with the campus health organization to further promote healthy eating and highlight the benefits of my product offerings. This collaborative effort proved to be a successful strategy, boosting sales significantly.

The results were fantastic! Students responded overwhelmingly to the healthier options, and my sales significantly increased. This experience highlights the importance of understanding your target audience and adapting your product offerings to meet their needs. By catering to the growing demand for healthy snacks, I was able to not only establish a loyal customer base but also contribute to promoting a healthier campus environment.

This story isn't unique. Another research published by Current Developments in Nutrition in 2020 also found that students are actively seeking healthier snack choices[viii].

While the idea of stocking your vending machines with exclusively healthy options might seem appealing, it's essential to approach this decision with careful consideration, as this was just my experience and observation for my business. While offering a variety of healthy snacks is undoubtedly beneficial, it's equally important to cater to the diverse preferences of your target audience.

My experience with the college campus location demonstrates the importance of understanding specific consumer needs. While students showed a preference for healthier options, they still enjoyed the occasional indulgence. Therefore, a balanced approach is crucial.

To effectively cater to your target market, conduct thorough research to identify their specific preferences. This involves observing consumer behavior, conducting surveys, and analyzing competitor offerings.

To identify your target audience:

Demographics

Age: Are you targeting college students, office workers, fitness enthusiasts, or the general population? For instance, a college campus may have a predominantly 18-24 age group, while a hospital setting will cater to a wider age range. For less obvious locations, observe the surroundings and foot traffic to estimate the age range. You can also use local census data or community surveys for more detailed insights.

To access local census data, you can start by visiting government websites such as the U.S. Census Bureau, which provides detailed demographic information. Many countries have similar official sites that offer census data. Additionally, local government offices and municipal planning departments often have specific demographic reports and data for your area. Local libraries and university research centers can also be valuable resources, as they typically provide access to census data through various databases and archives.

Gender: While not a definitive factor, understanding gender preferences can help tailor product offerings. For example, women might prefer healthier options, while men may lean towards more indulgent choices. Conducting surveys or analyzing sales data from similar locations can offer insights.

Income level: Consider the average income of your target audience. This will influence your pricing strategy and product selection. For instance, customers with higher disposable incomes might be willing to pay a premium for premium brands. In locations where income level is less obvious, consider the type of establishments nearby and the general affluence of the area. Local economic data or surveys can also provide valuable information.

Occupation: The occupation of your target audience can significantly impact their snacking habits. Office workers might prefer quick and convenient options, while students might seek more affordable choices. Observe the types of businesses and institutions in the area and gather feedback from local customers to get a clearer picture.

Behavioral Patterns

Observing customer behavior can provide valuable insights into their preferences and purchasing habits.

Shopping habits: Pay attention to when and how people buy snacks. Are they impulsive purchases or planned? Do they prefer self-service or cashier-operated options? You can perform direct observation at the location to learn about their shopping habits. Alternatively, gather data from industry reports and market research studies available online to see general trends or trends that are specific to your location.

Preferred products: Analyze the types of snacks and drinks popular in your target area through direct observation and sales data. Are there specific brands or categories that consistently outperform others?

Peak consumption times: Identify peak times for snack purchases by observing foot traffic and sales activity at different times of the day. Track the times when purchases are highest to optimize your product offerings and inventory management. For broader trends, consult market research reports or industry studies online or in libraries that provide insights into typical consumption patterns.

I always prefer to start with direct observation to gather firsthand data about customer behavior. Typically, I visit the location at different times of the day to capture various peak periods, staying for a few hours (sometimes, up to 3 hours) each visit to ensure a thorough understanding.

To avoid staying all day, I focus on specific times that are likely to be busiest (lunchtime, breaks, closing hour). I may visit the location multiple times (two weeks to one month) to build a comprehensive view before drawing any conclusions.

Sometimes, my direct observations may not align with online reports or library resources. In such cases, I always base my decisions on my own observations, as they provide the most accurate and relevant insights into the specific context.

Gathering Feedback

Directly engaging with your target audience is essential for gathering valuable feedback.

Surveys: Create surveys to collect data on customer preferences, purchasing habits, and desired product offerings. Offer incentives to encourage participation. For instance, you could offer a discount on their next purchase for completing the survey. This is what mine looks like:

Customer Preferences:

What types of snacks do you prefer to buy from vending machines? (Check all that apply)

- Chips
- Candy
- Healthy snacks (e.g., granola bars, nuts)

- Fresh fruits
- Beverages
- Other (please specify)

How often do you use vending machines?

- Daily
- Several times a week
- Weekly
- Monthly
- Rarely/Never

What time of day are you most likely to use a vending machine?

- Morning
- Afternoon
- Evening
- Late night

How important is the nutritional value of the snacks you purchase from vending machines?

- Very important
- Important
- Neutral
- Not very important
- Not important at all

What types of beverages do you prefer to purchase from vending machines? (Check all that apply)

- Water
- Soda
- Juice
- Energy drinks
- Coffee
- Tea
- Other (please specify)

Purchasing Habits:

How much do you typically spend on vending machine purchases per visit?

- Less than $1
- $1 - $2
- $2 - $3
- $3 - $5
- More than $5

What payment methods do you prefer to use at vending machines? (Check all that apply)

- Cash
- Credit/Debit card
- Mobile payment (e.g., Apple Pay, Google Wallet)

- Other (please specify)

Desired Product Offerings:

Are there any specific brands or products you would like to see in vending machines? (Please list)

1. ______
2. ______
3. ______
4. ______
5. ______

Would you be interested in purchasing healthy snack options if they were available in vending machines?

- Yes
- No
- Maybe

How likely are you to use a vending machine that offers fresh food options (e.g., sandwiches, salads)?

- Very Likely
- Likely
- Neutral
- Unlikely
- Very Unlikely

What factors influence your choice of snacks from vending machines?

- Price
- Taste
- Convenience
- Healthiness
- Other (please specify)

Interviews: Conduct one-on-one interviews with potential customers to gain deeper insights into their needs and expectations. Even though I haven't done a one-on-one interview, here are some potential interview questions:

- Can you describe your typical snacking habits?
- What do you look for in a vending machine?
- What kind of snacks would you like to see in vending machines?
- What prevents you from purchasing healthier options from vending machines?
- How important is price to you when choosing snacks?
- What do you like and dislike about vending machines?
- Have you ever been disappointed by the product selection in a vending machine? If so, what products were you hoping to find?
- How do you feel about the prices of items in vending machines? Do you find them reasonable or too high?

- What improvements would you like to see in the vending machines you use most often?
- Would you be willing to pay a premium for higher-quality or healthier products in vending machines? Why or why not?
- How do you think vending machines could better meet your needs or fit into your daily routine?
- Do you have any concerns about the freshness or quality of products from vending machines? If so, what are they?
- Would you prefer vending machines that offer more local or specialty products? Why or why not?
- How important is it to you that vending machines offer environmentally friendly or sustainable products?

Observation: Spend time observing customer behavior at nearby stores or vending machines. Pay attention to what products they choose and how they interact with the vending machines. Here is what to look for:

Product Selection:

- **Popular Items:** Notice which products are most frequently chosen by customers. Are there certain snacks, drinks, or other items that are more popular?
- **Ignored Items:** Identify products that are consistently overlooked. This can indicate what products might not be worth stocking.

- **Variety Preference:** Observe if customers prefer a wide variety of options or if they tend to choose from a limited selection of familiar products.

Interaction with the Vending Machine:

- **Ease of Use:** Watch how easily customers operate the vending machine. Are there any signs of frustration or confusion?
- **Payment Methods:** Notice what payment methods are most commonly used. Are customers using cash, cards, or mobile payments?
- **Time Spent:** Measure how long customers spend at the vending machine from the moment they arrive to when they walk away.

Buying Patterns:

- **Time of Day:** Observe during different times of the day to see when the vending machine gets the most traffic.
- **Frequency of Use:** Notice if there are repeat customers and how often they use the machine.
- **Quantity of Purchases:** Pay attention to whether customers are buying single items or multiple items in one visit.

Customer Reactions:

- **Satisfaction Level:** Look for visible signs of satisfaction or dissatisfaction, such as smiles, frowns, or verbal comments.

- **Feedback:** If customers discuss their purchases with others nearby, listen to what they say about the products and the vending machine experience.

Tips for Effective Observation

- Be Inconspicuous: Try to blend in and avoid drawing attention to yourself. This ensures you observe natural customer behavior.
- Take Notes: Keep a small notebook or use a mobile device to jot down observations in real-time.
- Vary Observation Times: Spend time observing at different times of the day and week to get a comprehensive understanding of customer behavior.
- Look for Patterns: After multiple observation sessions, review your notes to identify common patterns and trends.

By combining demographic data, behavioral analysis, and direct customer feedback, you can create a detailed profile of your target audience. This information will serve as the foundation for making informed decisions about your business.

Analyzing Competitors

Understanding your competitors is another crucial step. Look at what other vending machine businesses in your area are doing. What products do they offer? What prices are they charging? Are their machines placed in high-traffic locations? Analyzing these factors can give you an edge.

Remember the other machine I placed in a corporate office building? As you may recall, sales were low, below my $400/month goal. As I would later discover, the reason for the low and slow sales were because another vending machine nearby offered similar products at slightly lower prices. I realized I needed to differentiate my offerings. After analyzing my competitor, I introduced premium products like organic snacks and specialty coffees. This move attracted a different customer segment, and my sales increased by 30% in just three months.

To analyze your competitors:

Product Range

- **Identify Competitors:** Determine who your primary competitors are in your target locations. This includes other vending machine operators, convenience stores, or campus cafeterias. Visit these locations to see firsthand what they offer and how they operate. As a general rule, competitors are those within a close radius, usually within a 1 to 2-mile range, depending on the area's density and traffic.
- **Analyze Product Offerings:** Observe the types of products your competitors sell. Pay attention to the variety, quality, and pricing of their items. Take note of any popular or unique products that draw customer interest.

- **Identify Gaps:** Look for product categories that are underrepresented or absent from your competitors' offerings. This could indicate opportunities to fill a niche in the market. For instance, if competitors mainly offer sugary snacks, introducing a range of healthy options could attract customers looking for healthier choices.

Pricing Strategy

- **Competitive pricing:** Research the prices of similar products offered by your competitors. This will help you establish a competitive price point for your own products.
- **Value proposition:** Consider the perceived value of your products. If you offer higher-quality or healthier options, you might justify a slightly higher price point. Compare your products directly with competitors to determine if the added value supports a higher price.
- **Promotional pricing:** Experiment with limited-time discounts or promotions to attract new customers and generate interest. Track the effectiveness of these promotions compared to competitors' pricing strategies. To track the effectiveness of your discounts or promotions, start by setting clear goals and metrics for evaluation. Monitor sales data during the promotion period and compare it with sales data from before and after the promotion. Observe the number of new customers and repeat

purchases (possible with only card-enabled machines), and use customer feedback to gauge their response. Additionally, analyze how these promotional sales figures compare to competitors' pricing strategies to determine if the promotion increased your market share or customer engagement. Implementing a system to record these metrics, such as sales tracking software or a spreadsheet, can help assess the overall impact of your promotional efforts.

Location Analysis

- **High-traffic areas:** Identify locations with high foot traffic, such as college campuses, office buildings, hospitals, and transportation hubs. Visiting these locations helps assess the potential demand and competition.
- **Competition analysis:** Assess the number of existing vending machines in your target locations. Look for areas with limited competition or opportunities to offer unique products.
- **Customer demographics:** Consider the demographics of the people frequenting different locations. Tailor your product offerings accordingly. For example, a gym might benefit from protein bars and energy drinks, while a hospital could have a higher demand for healthier options.

By carefully analyzing your competitors, you can develop a competitive advantage and increase your chances of success in the vending machine business.

Finding the Best Locations for Your Machines

Location is key in the vending machine business. Placing your machines in high-traffic areas ensures maximum visibility and usage. In my personal experience, doing this business for two years with 50 machines across Atlanta, I can boldly say that vending machines placed in schools, hospitals, gyms, airports, and office buildings report the highest sales volumes.

When I scouted locations for my machines, I visited potential spots at different times of the day to gauge foot traffic. One of my most successful placements was in a 24-hour gym. Gyms are great because people often crave quick, healthy snacks and drinks after their workouts. By placing a machine stocked with protein bars, sports drinks, and other fitness-related snacks, I saw consistent sales throughout the day and night.

Steps to find the best locations:

- **High-Traffic Areas:** Look for places where people frequently pass by or gather.
- **Accessibility:** Ensure your machines are easy to reach and not hidden.

- **Permission:** Secure agreements with property owners or managers.

For instance, when placing machines in office buildings, I made sure to meet with property managers to negotiate placement and electricity access. In one case, I offered a small percentage of the profits to the building management, which secured me a prime location in the lobby.

In conclusion, understanding your target audience is crucial, but equally important is pinpointing the ideal locations for your vending machines. This requires careful consideration of factors such as foot traffic, competition, and the specific needs of your target market.

Chapter five will reveal more about location selection, providing a comprehensive list of potential locations and factors to consider. We'll explore everything from high-traffic areas to niche markets, providing you with a detailed analysis of various location types and strategies to maximize your business potential.

Up next: We'll talk about the various types of vending machines, their features, and factors to consider when making a purchase.

CHAPTER 4:
Choosing the Right Vending Machines

Choosing the right vending machines is one of the most important steps in building a successful business. The type of machine you choose will determine the products you can sell, the locations where you can place them, and ultimately, how much profit you can make.

When I first began this venture, I dedicated countless hours to researching different types of vending machines. Online resources were helpful, but I knew I needed firsthand experience to truly understand the differences. Although I had previously encountered a few machines, I hadn't paid much attention to their features because the business didn't catch my interest back then.

It wasn't until I became serious about the business that I started to notice and actively seek out the unique qualities and similarities in various machines. My focus shifted from simply recognizing a vending machine to understanding what made each one stand out.

I remember visiting various locations and studying the types of machines in operation. At that point, it wasn't just about observing the machines themselves; I was curious about their placement, the products offered, and the overall customer interaction. There were times when I saw a particular type of vending machine I had never seen before. The temptation to purchase a product, even if I didn't need it, was irresistible simply to experience the vending process firsthand.

This hands-on approach allowed me to gain valuable insights into the strengths and weaknesses of different machine types. I learned about the importance of factors such as product capacity, payment options, and energy efficiency. With this practical knowledge, I was able to make informed decisions about the vending machines that best suit my business goals. Or, did I? We'll see.

Types of Vending Machines

The world of vending machines is vast and varied, offering a plethora of choices for entrepreneurs. From classic snack and beverage dispensers to more specialized options, understanding the different types available is essential for making informed decisions. Through my extensive research and hands-on experience, I've identified several primary types of vending machines:

Snack Vending Machines: These are the most common type, dispensing a variety of snacks such as chips, candy, cookies, and granola bars. They come in different sizes to accommodate various product selections. Popular models include the Seaga Infinity INF5S, AMS Sensit 3, and Vendo V21. The Seaga Infinity INF5S is known for its user-friendly interface and holds up to 547 snack items, making it ideal for high-traffic locations. The AMS Sensit 3 stands out for its energy efficiency and adjustable shelving, accommodating a large variety of products. The Vendo V21 is durable and easy to maintain, with a capacity of up to 550 items, making it perfect for mid-sized locations. These models provide different features to suit your business needs, from compact machines for smaller spaces to larger units for areas with higher demand.

Beverage Vending Machines: Designed for cold drinks, these machines typically offer a combination of carbonated beverages, juices, water, and energy drinks. Look for models with advanced cooling systems to maintain product freshness. Specific models like the Dixie Narco BevMax 4, Vendo Vue 30, and Royal Vendors RVV 500 are excellent options in this category. The Dixie Narco BevMax 4 is popular for its large glass front, which allows customers to easily view and select from up to 45 different beverages, making it ideal for locations with high foot traffic. The Vendo Vue 30 offers energy-efficient cooling and can dispense a wide variety of drink sizes, while the Royal Vendors RVV 500 is known for its durability and advanced temperature control, accommodating up to 500 cans or bottles. These models are designed to meet diverse customer preferences, ensuring you can provide a wide range of beverage options while maintaining product quality and freshness.

Combo Vending Machines: These machines combine both snacks and beverages in a single unit, offering convenience for customers. However, they often have limitations in terms of product variety and capacity. It's essential to assess whether the benefits of a combo machine outweigh the potential drawbacks for your specific business needs. Brands like Seaga and AMS (Automated Merchandising Systems) offer reliable combo machines. The Seaga Infinity INF5C is a popular model known for its flexibility and customizable configurations, allowing operators to adjust the machine layout to include both snacks and drinks. The AMS Snack & Drink Combo machine is another great option, featuring Sensit technology that ensures products are dispensed properly and offers an intuitive interface for easy selection. These models are well-suited for locations with moderate traffic where space is limited, providing a balanced selection of snacks and beverages to meet diverse customer preferences.

Hot Food Vending Machines: For more ambitious entrepreneurs, hot food vending machines offer the opportunity to expand your product line. These machines require advanced technology to keep food at optimal temperatures. Consider factors like energy consumption, maintenance requirements, and the availability of suitable food options when choosing a hot food vending machine. Brands like USelectIt and Crane have developed reliable models for this market. The USelectIt Evoke Hot Food Vending Machine is known for its efficient heating system and user-friendly interface, making it a solid choice for serving items like sandwiches, burgers, and pizza. Another popular model is the Crane Shopper 2, which offers a wide selection of hot meals and snacks, with features that maintain consistent temperatures and ensure easy loading and restocking.

Cold Food Vending Machines: This emerging trend caters to the increasing demand for fresh and healthy food options. These machines dispense pre-packaged salads, sandwiches, yogurt, and other refrigerated items. The Seaga Infinity INF5C is a notable model, known for its high-capacity storage and customizable configurations, allowing operators to offer a diverse selection of fresh food items. Another excellent choice is the AMS Healthy Vend model, which provides superior cooling capabilities and easy-to-use features, ensuring that products remain fresh and appealing.

Smart Vending Machines: These state-of-the-art machines incorporate technology to enhance the customer experience and provide valuable data insights. Features may include digital displays, cashless payment options, product tracking, and even personalized recommendations. While these machines tend to be more expensive, they can offer a competitive advantage. The Vengo Labs vending machine is a prime example, featuring compact designs and digital displays that engage users while offering cashless payment options through mobile wallets and credit cards. Another standout model is the Crane Media2, which offers a large interactive touchscreen, product tracking capabilities, and real-time inventory management. These machines are equipped with technologies that provide personalized product recommendations based on purchasing patterns, enhancing customer satisfaction and boosting sales. Although smart vending machines often come with a higher price tag, their ability to deliver detailed analytics and an engaging user interface can offer a significant competitive advantage in the market.

Bulk Vending Machines: Ideal for dispensing small items like candy, gum, or nuts in high-traffic areas such as malls, theaters, and family entertainment centers. The Beaver Machine Corporation offers the popular "Round Beaver" series, known for its durability and reliability. These machines feature a large capacity and a robust coin mechanism, making them a cost-effective choice for operators. The "LYPC Pro" series is another reliable option, offering models with adjustable dispensing wheels to accommodate various product sizes. Both brands provide a wide variety of models that can be customized to fit specific needs, ensuring they can handle large quantities of products while maintaining ease of use and maintenance.

Gumball and Novelty Machines: Primarily targeting children and young adults, these machines offer a fun and engaging experience. They often feature colorful designs and a variety of toy or candy options. One popular brand is Northwestern, which offers the "Super 60" series, known for its sturdy build and eye-catching appearance. These machines can dispense both gumballs and small novelty toys, making them versatile options for entertainment venues. The "VendMaster" series by Rhino is another well-regarded option, featuring customizable designs and the ability to dispense a variety of small items. These machines are often equipped with playful graphics and can be placed in locations like amusement parks, arcades, and family-friendly restaurants.

Custom Vending Machines: For businesses with unique product offerings, custom vending machines can be tailored to specific needs. These machines can dispense anything from electronics to pharmaceuticals to beauty products to fresh flowers. Companies like U-Select-It provide customizable models that can be adapted for various items. The "Mercato 5000" model is popular for its flexibility, allowing for the adjustment of shelving and compartments to accommodate different product sizes and shapes. These machines offer businesses the ability to create a specialized vending experience, ensuring that the machine fits their particular product requirements while also maintaining reliability and ease of use.

Beyond the primary vending machine types above, there's a growing market for specialized machines that cater to specific consumer segments and preferences.

Pizza Vending Machines: Providing freshly prepared pizza slices, these machines cater to the on-the-go consumer seeking a quick and satisfying meal. College campuses, office buildings, and entertainment venues are potential locations. One prominent example is the "Let's Pizza" machine, which crafts pizzas from scratch, including kneading the dough and adding toppings, all within minutes. Popular across Europe, it provides a fast, fresh option for those in need of a quick meal. Another innovative model is the "Pizza ATM" by Paline, which stores up to 70 pre-made pizzas and bakes them to order in about three minutes, offering convenience and quality, particularly on college campuses. Additionally, "Piestro" presents a robotic solution that assembles and bakes customizable pizzas on demand, making it perfect for entertainment venues where swift service is essential. These machines are designed to deliver quick, satisfying meals, catering to the fast-paced needs of today's consumers.

Hamburger Vending Machines: Offering a classic fast-food option, these machines can be successful in locations with high foot traffic and a demand for quick meals. One notable example is the

RoboBurger, which grills and assembles burgers fresh to order in just a few minutes. It's ideal for locations such as airports, malls, and office buildings, where people are looking for a quick, hot meal. These machines cater to the fast-paced lifestyle of modern consumers, delivering freshly prepared burgers efficiently and consistently.

Ice Vending Machines: Provides a convenient solution for time-pressed consumers, making them ideal for residential areas, college campuses, and busy transportation hubs. A standout in this category is Ice House America vending machines, which deliver fresh, bagged ice 24/7. These machines are perfect for residential communities and outdoor event venues, ensuring a reliable supply of ice whenever needed. They cater to the fast-paced lifestyle of modern consumers, offering an efficient and accessible solution for quick refreshment needs.

Ice Cream Vending Machines: Perfect for hot summer days, these machines offer a refreshing treat for all ages. Beachfronts, parks, and amusement parks are ideal locations. One notable brand is the NISSEI Ice Cream Vending Machine, which provides a wide variety of ice cream flavors and styles, making it a popular choice for beachfronts and parks. Another model is the FastCorp Z400 Series, known for its ability to store and dispense various ice cream products efficiently, making it ideal for amusement parks where quick service is essential. These machines provide a delightful solution for cooling down and enjoying a sweet treat in popular outdoor locations.

Cupcake Vending Machines: Catering to the sweet tooth, these machines offer a decadent indulgence. Suitable for high-traffic areas with a focus on impulse purchases. A popular example is the Sprinkles Cupcake ATM, known for its eye-catching design and ability to dispense freshly baked cupcakes 24/7, making it ideal for shopping malls and urban centers. Another model is the Baked by Melissa Cupcake Vending Machine, which provides a variety of mini cupcakes, allowing consumers to enjoy different flavors in one purchase.

Raw Milk Vending Machines: Targeting health-conscious consumers seeking fresh, unpasteurized milk. Ideal for locations with a strong focus on organic and natural products. One notable brand is the DF Italia Milk Vending Machine, which dispenses raw milk sourced directly from local farms, ensuring freshness and quality. Another model is the RistoMilk Vending Machine by Risto Europe, known for its user-friendly interface and ability to maintain the optimal temperature for preserving milk quality.

Breathalyzer Vending Machines: Targeting safety-conscious individuals, these machines are often found in bars, clubs, and designated driving areas. One prominent model is the BACtrack Vending Machine, which provides users with access to accurate breathalyzer tests to measure blood alcohol content. Another example is the AlcoSense Vending Machine, designed for use in nightlife venues and transportation hubs, offering a convenient way for individuals to check their sobriety before driving. These machines promote safety by providing easy access to breathalyzer testing in high-risk areas.

Condom Vending Machines: Promoting sexual health, these machines are typically placed in healthcare facilities, universities, hotels, or entertainment venues. One notable model is the Haleon Condom Vending Machine, which offers a range of condom types and sizes, ensuring accessibility in places like universities and healthcare centers. Another example is the Condom Sense Vending Machine, designed for use in hotels and entertainment venues, providing discreet access to condoms for guests and visitors.

Gold to Go Vending Machines: Offering small amounts of gold as an investment option, these machines target a specific niche market. One notable example is the Gold ATM by Gold & Co., which provides a range of gold products, including coins and bars, catering to investors and collectors looking for convenient access to precious metals. These machines are typically placed in high-end retail locations and luxury hotels, appealing to those interested in gold investment.

New Versus Used Machines

When buying a Vending Machine, you might want to consider buying a used machine as an alternative to buying a new machine. However, the decision to purchase a new or used vending machine involves weighing several factors, which we will discuss below.

New Vending Machines

Advantages: New machines offer the latest technology, including energy-efficient components, advanced payment systems, and user-friendly interfaces. They often come with comprehensive warranties that provide peace of mind. Additionally, new machines typically have a longer lifespan and require less maintenance in the short term.

Costs: The price of a new vending machine can vary significantly based on size, features, and brand. Expect to invest anywhere from a few thousand dollars to tens of thousands for a high-end model. Popular brands in the industry include Crane, Seaga, and Vendstar, known for their reliability and innovation.

Purchasing Options: New vending machines can be purchased directly from manufacturers, distributors, or authorized dealers. Research different brands, compare features, and request quotes to find the best deal that aligns with your budget and business needs. Consider factors such as shipping costs, installation services, and warranty terms when making your decision.

Used Vending Machines

Advantages: Used vending machines offer a more budget-friendly entry point into the vending business. They can be purchased at a fraction of the cost of a new machine, allowing you to allocate more funds towards inventory, marketing, or additional machines.

Disadvantages: Used machines may require additional investments in repairs and maintenance. They might also lack the latest technology and energy-efficient features.

Purchasing Options: Used vending machines can be found through online marketplaces, classified ads, or directly from other vending machine operators. When purchasing a used machine, it's essential to inspect it thoroughly for signs of wear and tear. Request maintenance records and consider hiring a technician to assess its condition.

Assessing a Used Machine's History:

To ensure you're making a sound investment, gather as much information as possible about the machine's history. Ask the seller for maintenance records, repair history, and any available documentation. If possible, contact previous owners to inquire about the machine's performance and reliability.

My Personal Experience on Buying Machine

Up until the moment I approached the seller, everything I knew was just theoretical. In practice, selecting the ideal vending machine was a learning curve for me. Initially, I approached the task with a sense of overconfidence, assuming I had a basic understanding of the machines. I studied different types of vending machines, compared features, and read countless reviews. I felt ready to make a purchase, convinced I knew exactly what I was doing. But when I walked into that showroom and saw the machines lined up, something unexpected happened—I forgot everything I had learned.

It was as if my brain went on autopilot, and I was drawn to the first machine that caught my eye. It was a beauty, gleaming under the showroom lights. This vending machine was a masterpiece of design, with a sleek, modern exterior and glossy panels that reflected the light like a diamond. The bright colors and digital display were mesmerizing, promising a futuristic experience. I was captivated by its aesthetic appeal as if it were a shiny new car.

The machine had all sorts of unnecessary features—LED lights that changed colors, a touch screen with animated graphics, and even built-in speakers that played music. It looked brand new, but it was actually refurbished. None of these features were crucial to functionality, yet I was smitten. It was hard to resist something so dazzling. The practical considerations faded from my mind. I was like a magpie drawn to shiny objects, utterly forgetting the importance of choosing a functional machine.

I should have remembered that substance trumps style, but I was too caught up in the allure of that machine. Its exterior was flawless, free of dents or scratches, and it had a presence that made it stand out from the rest. I imagined it in a prime location, attracting customers with its sophisticated appearance. In fact, I was convinced that its appearance alone would captivate passersby, leading them to make impulse purchases purely based on the machine's eye-catching charm. Unfortunately, I ignored the most important lesson I'd learned: looks aren't everything.

That was one of my earliest missteps! I purchased a used machine without conducting a thorough inspection. While the initial cost savings seemed attractive, I soon discovered hidden maintenance issues that resulted in unexpected expenses and downtime. At first, everything seemed fine. The machine functioned well for a few weeks, but then problems began to surface.

The machine started making strange noises, and some of the shelves jammed, refusing to dispense products. I was flooded with complaints from customers who didn't receive their purchases. This situation was not only frustrating but also embarrassing for my business. I had to shut down the machine for repairs, leading to a significant loss of revenue.

The downtime lasted nearly a month as I struggled to find the right parts and a technician who could fix it. Every day felt like a battle, and my frustration grew. I decided to contact the seller to vent my anger.

I picked up the phone, feeling a mix of frustration and determination. "Hello, this is Lena Voss," I said, trying to keep my voice steady. "I bought a vending machine from you a few weeks ago, and it's been nothing but trouble. The shelves jam, the noise it makes is unbearable, and I've lost so much business because of this."

The seller responded with a calm tone. "I'm sorry to hear that, Ms. Voss. We do our best to refurbish our machines to the highest standards. Have you tried checking the sensors? Sometimes, a simple adjustment can solve the problem."

"Checking the sensors?" I replied, struggling to maintain my composure. "I didn't pay for a fixer-upper project. I need a reliable machine, not something that breaks down every other day. What are you going to do about it?"

The seller paused, then said, "I understand your frustration. Let me arrange for a technician to visit your location and take a closer look. We'll ensure the machine is up and running as soon as possible."

After multiple attempts to repair the machine and get it back in working order, it became clear that my initial purchase was not going to pay off. Each fix seemed to only lead to another breakdown, and the unreliability was frustrating both me and my customers. It was like a domino effect; as soon as one issue was resolved, another popped up.

By the third month after purchase, the situation had become untenable. Despite the seller's assurances and the technician's repeated visits, the vending machine continued to malfunction. The shelves still jammed occasionally, the digital display flickered erratically, and the noise persisted. The time and money I had spent trying to maintain this machine were adding up, with no end in sight.

I reached a breaking point one particularly hectic afternoon when I received yet another call from a customer who had lost their purchase on a jammed shelf. I could hear the frustration in their voice, and it mirrored my own feelings. At that moment, I realized I needed to cut my losses and make a decisive move.

I contacted the seller once again, but this time with a firm decision. "I'm sorry, but I can’t continue with this machine," I told them. "It's been one problem after another, and I've lost too much time and business because of it. I need to return it."

The seller, to their credit, was understanding. "We apologize for the inconvenience, Ms. Voss. We'll arrange for the machine to be picked up and process your return."

This experience underscored the importance of due diligence when buying used equipment. I realized that I should have taken the time to inspect the machine thoroughly, perhaps even brought along an expert to ensure everything was in working order.

Conversely, I also learned the value of investing in quality. While a higher upfront cost might be tempting to avoid, a reliable machine with advanced features can often lead to increased sales and reduced maintenance expenses in the long run. My experience taught me that cutting corners might save money initially, but it often leads to greater expenses down the road.

Remember, when it comes to vending machines, the saying "don't judge a book by its cover" couldn't be more accurate. Look beyond the surface, and make decisions based on practicality, not just aesthetics.

Determined to avoid repeating the same mistakes, I decided to invest in a brand-new vending machine from a reputable supplier. This time, I did my homework thoroughly, examining various options and prioritizing quality, reliability, and customer service.

The new supplier I chose came highly recommended by fellow entrepreneurs in the vending business. Their machines were known for their durability and cutting-edge features that enhanced both the owner and customer experience. After evaluating my options, I finally settled on a model that, while more expensive upfront, promised fewer headaches in the long run.

The moment the new machine was delivered, I could tell it was a step up from my previous purchase. It was sleek, modern, and sturdy, with an intuitive interface and customizable shelving to accommodate a wide range of products. The machine was equipped with the latest technology, including a state-of-the-art digital display and advanced payment systems that accepted contactless and mobile payments, meeting the demands of today's consumers.

From the start, the new vending machine performed flawlessly. It quickly became a favorite among my customers, who appreciated the seamless transactions and reliable service. I noticed an uptick in sales as customers felt more confident in their purchases without the fear of a jam or malfunction.

Maintaining the machine became a straightforward part of my routine. Instead of scrambling to address breakdowns, I focused on preventative maintenance—checking on its condition, refilling products, and ensuring the payment systems were operating smoothly. This proactive approach kept the machine in top condition, allowing it to function optimally and serve my customers without interruptions.

The peace of mind that came with this new machine was invaluable. I no longer had to worry about unexpected repairs or downtime. Instead, I could focus on expanding my business and exploring new opportunities.

I want to emphasize that my experience with the used vending machine is not meant to discourage you from considering pre-owned equipment. In fact, buying used machines can be a smart and cost-effective strategy if approached correctly. This is about learning from my early mistakes and equipping you with the knowledge to make better choices.

There are many excellent used vending machines available that can offer great value and performance. Since that initial setback, I have successfully purchased many used machines, which now make up a significant portion of my vending fleet. These machines have proven to be reliable, efficient, and profitable investments.

The key to purchasing a used vending machine is knowing what to look for and conducting a thorough evaluation before making a purchase. Below, you will learn about the critical factors you should consider, including inspecting the machine's condition, understanding its maintenance history, and ensuring it meets your specific business needs.

When done right, investing in used vending machines can allow you to expand your business while managing costs effectively. By sharing my journey and the lessons I've learned, I hope to help you make informed decisions that will set you up for success in your vending machine business. Whether you choose new or used, the important thing is to approach each purchase with diligence and foresight.

Key Features to Look For

When selecting vending machines, whether new or used, certain features are crucial to ensure optimal performance and customer satisfaction. Drawing from my years of experience in this industry, I've identified the following key features that can make or break your vending business.

Reliability

In the vending machine business, reliability is non-negotiable. A machine that frequently breaks down not only frustrates customers but also leads to lost revenue. Early in my career, I made the mistake of choosing a cheaper, lesser-known brand to cut costs, only to find myself constantly dealing with breakdowns and unhappy customers. That experience taught me that investing in reliable machines is worth every penny. Over the years, I've found that certain brands have consistently outperformed others. For instance, machines from AMS and Seaga have shown remarkable durability and require minimal maintenance. These brands have been staples in my fleet, particularly models like the AMS 39 VCF for snacks and the Seaga Infinity series for beverages. Their components are built to last, and their failure rates are among the lowest in the industry.

Capacity

Choosing the right capacity for your vending machine is all about balancing the needs of your market with the space you have available. When I first placed a machine in a busy hospital, I underestimated the demand and chose a model with limited capacity. It wasn't long before I realized my mistake—the machine was constantly running out of stock, leading to missed sales opportunities. I quickly upgraded to a Vendo 721, which holds up to 680 12-oz cans, and saw a significant improvement in both sales and customer satisfaction. On the other hand, for a smaller setting like a boutique gym, a machine like the Seaga HY900, which has a capacity of 240 items, might be more appropriate. This allows you to offer a curated selection without wasting space on a machine that's too large.

Payment Options

In today's cashless society, offering multiple payment methods is essential. I remember a time when one of my machines was only equipped to accept cash, and I noticed it wasn't performing as well as expected. After some research, I learned that many of my customers in that area preferred to pay with credit cards or mobile payments. I decided to upgrade the machine to include options like Apple Pay and Google Wallet, and the difference was night and day. Sales increased almost immediately, especially in locations frequented by younger, tech-savvy consumers. Machines like the Crane National 449 and the Seaga N2G4000 are equipped with advanced payment systems that accept a variety of methods, making them versatile for different customer preferences.

Security Features

Protecting your investment is critical, especially in areas prone to vandalism or theft. I'll never forget the time one of my machines was targeted by vandals—it was a wake-up call to the importance of robust security features. After that incident, I switched to machines with reinforced steel cabinets, tamper-proof coin mechanisms, and alarm systems. For instance, the AMS 39 Snack Machine is equipped with a dual-pane glass door that's more resistant to break-ins, and the Seaga VC630 comes with an alarm system that triggers when the door is forced open. These features have been instrumental in reducing theft and damage to my machines, saving both time and money on repairs.

Energy Efficiency

Energy costs can add up quickly, especially if you're operating a large number of machines. I learned this the hard way when I received an unexpectedly high electricity bill one month. That's when I started looking into energy-efficient models. Opting for machines with ENERGY STAR certification, like the Crane Merchant Media series, can significantly reduce your operating expenses. These machines use up to 30% less energy compared to non-certified models. This not only helps your bottom line but also aligns with the growing consumer preference for environmentally-friendly businesses. Over time, the savings on energy costs can be substantial, making energy efficiency a feature worth prioritizing.

Maintenance and Repair

No matter how reliable a machine is, occasional maintenance and repairs are inevitable. Early on, I didn't pay much attention to this aspect, and when a machine broke down, I found myself scrambling to find the right parts and a qualified technician. Now, I make it a point to choose machines with readily available spare parts and strong technical support from the manufacturer or distributor. Brands like Crane and AMS offer extensive networks of authorized service centers and parts suppliers, making it easy to keep your machines in top working condition. I've found that having a reliable source for parts and repairs can drastically reduce downtime, keeping my machines operational and profitable.

Selecting the right vending machine involves more than just picking a model off the shelf. It's about understanding your market, knowing what features matter most, and investing in machines that offer reliability, security, and efficiency. From my experience, the machines you choose can set the tone for your entire business, so take the time to make informed decisions. With the right equipment, you'll be well on your way to building a profitable and sustainable vending machine business.

Up next: We will talk extensively about the art and science of location selection. You will learn everything from high-traffic areas and negotiation tactics to legal considerations and permit requirements. Are you ready to discover the secrets to finding the most profitable spots for your vending machines?

CHAPTER 5:
Finding and Securing Locations

As an entrepreneur with a background in digital marketing, the concept of high traffic is ingrained in my business philosophy. Driving traffic to landing pages and optimizing conversion rates are fundamental to online success. Similarly, in the vending machine business, location is paramount.

High foot traffic equates to increased visibility and potential customers. Just as my digital marketing strategies rely on numbers to measure success, the vending machine business thrives on the power of location and volume. Strategic placement in high-traffic areas, such as college campuses, office buildings, or transportation hubs, can significantly impact sales and overall profitability.

In my experience, locations with over 300 daily visitors are ideal for placing vending machines. This amount of foot traffic is usually enough to sustain regular sales. When choosing a location, I've found it important to consider the demographics of the area and the type of products you offer. For instance, a gym would benefit from a vending machine stocked with protein bars and energy drinks, while a college campus might require a wider variety of snacks and beverages.

One of my first placements was a busy gym in the heart of Atlanta. I chose it because fitness enthusiasts often look for quick and healthy snacks post-workout, and the gym has hundreds of daily visitors. This choice turned out to be a goldmine! Keep in mind that while large volumes of foot traffic can boost sales, each location can have unique advantages and challenges. Here are some of the best high-traffic locations, along with other information.

Note that: while some of the examples and statistics provided in this section may be focused on the United States (sometimes, Atlanta, to be precise), the principles of identifying high-traffic areas apply universally.

Airports

Airports are bustling hubs with thousands of travelers and staff passing through daily. These locations provide a captive audience eager for convenient snacks and drinks between flights or while waiting for transportation. The constant flow of passengers, who are often in transit and looking for quick refreshments, creates a strong demand for vending machine products. Take Hartsfield-Jackson Atlanta International Airport, for instance. With an average of 286,000 passengers passing through daily and over 2,100 arrivals and departures, the foot traffic is unparalleled[ix]. It's important to note that this figure doesn't even account for the airport's staff, which further increases the potential customer base.

Pros: The 24/7 nature of airports means constant foot traffic, providing a steady flow of potential customers.

Cons: High competition and potential exclusivity agreements with existing vendors. High leasing fees or revenue-sharing demands from airport management can significantly impact profit margins.

Identification: Understandably, not all airports are the same in terms of foot traffic. For your city, begin your research by looking at airports with high passenger traffic. You can do this by checking airport websites, the aviation body in your country, and industry reports like those from Airports Council International to obtain detailed passenger statistics.

Bus and Train Stations

Like airports, bus and train stations have a high volume of daily commuters and travelers. Many people use public transportation for daily commutes, making these locations ideal for vending machines offering quick, on-the-go options. A report from the American Public Transportation Association noted that public transit systems in the U.S. provided approximately 9.9 billion rides in 2019, and 34 million times each weekday, people board public transportation[x]. Major stations can see thousands of visitors per day.

Pros: Regular commuter traffic, particularly during peak travel hours. Lower overhead costs compared to airports.

Cons: Varying levels of foot traffic depending on the station's size and location. Security concerns may arise in certain areas.

Identification: Look for stations in major metropolitan areas with high daily ridership. The American Public Transportation Association and individual transit authorities often publish ridership statistics. Apart from looking at information provided by the transportation board in your city, you could visit these stations individually to observe the foot traffic. As I mentioned in the introduction of this chapter, locations with over 300 daily visitors are ideal.

Hospitals and Care Facilities

Hospitals and care facilities have a steady stream of visitors, patients, and staff. These individuals often require snacks and drinks during long waiting periods or shifts, making vending machines a valuable convenience. The American Hospital Association reported that there are around 6,120 hospitals in the U.S., serving millions of patients annually[xi]. High-traffic hospitals can have over 2,000 visitors daily.

Pros: Consistent traffic from patients, visitors, and staff. Demand for food options around the clock, particularly in facilities that operate 24/7.

Cons: Potential restrictions on the types of products that can be sold, particularly related to health regulations.

Identification: Start by looking at the largest hospitals in your city or those with high bed counts. Check government health directories and hospital websites for information. The American Hospital Association provides a directory of hospitals, including key statistics.

Warehouses

Warehouses employ large numbers of workers who often need quick and accessible food and beverage options during breaks. Vending machines in these settings cater to employees working long shifts, particularly in locations where food services are limited. According to

DATA USA, the warehousing and storage sector employed over 1.3 million people in 2023, with facilities typically operating 24/7[xii].

Pros: Large, concentrated workforce needing quick meal options during breaks. Typically, lower competition compared to public-facing locations.

Cons: Limited customer base confined to the workforce; potentially lower overall sales compared to public areas.

Identification: Focus on areas with large industrial parks or logistics hubs. You can check online resources, contact local representatives, and subscribe to relevant publications to gather information on industrial properties, their size, occupancy rates, and economic activity in your city.

Office Buildings

Office buildings are filled with professionals who appreciate convenient access to snacks and beverages throughout the workday. Vending machines in office settings provide quick options for busy employees who may not have time to leave the premises. Statista reported that as of September 2024, there were 134.15 million full-time employees in the United States. This is a slight decrease from the previous month when there were 134.4 million full-time employees[xiii]. Most of these employees work in office environments with hundreds of occupants in a single building.

Pros: Steady demand for snacks and beverages throughout the workday. Often easier to secure long-term contracts.

Cons: Traffic can fluctuate based on the workweek, with lower sales on weekends.

Identification: Look for multi-tenant office buildings in busy business districts. Commercial real estate firms often publish occupancy rates and tenant information.

Apartment Complexes

Apartment complexes offer a concentrated residential audience that benefits from easy access to vending machines. Tenants appreciate the convenience of grabbing a snack or drink without leaving the property, especially during late hours. In 2022, Multi Family Dive stated there are over 20 million apartment units in the U.S., housing over 36 million residents[xiv]. That number has only increased since then and will continue to grow!

Pros: Captive residential audience with potential for regular, repeat customers. Convenient access for tenants, especially for late-night snacks.

Cons: Limited to the building's residents, which may cap the sales potential.

Identification: Focus on large complexes with high occupancy rates. Real estate websites and property management companies can offer insights into tenant demographics and complex sizes.

Dealerships

Car dealerships have visitors who spend significant time waiting during car purchases, maintenance, or services. Vending machines can serve both customers and employees, providing refreshments in a setting where foot traffic can be unpredictable. The National Automobile Dealers Association reported over 16,800 franchised dealerships in the U.S., selling 7.6 million vehicles in 2023[xv].

Pros: Customers spend considerable time at dealerships during car buying or servicing, creating demand for snacks and drinks.

Cons: Foot traffic can be inconsistent, depending on the day or season.

Identification: Target high-volume dealerships with substantial customer service areas. Industry reports and local business directories can help you to identify top-performing dealerships.

Hotels

Hotels accommodate travelers who often seek convenient snacks and drinks, especially after restaurant hours. Vending machines in hotel lobbies or common areas provide 24/7 access for guests and staff alike.

According to the American Hotel & Lodging Association, there are over 54,000 hotel properties in the U.S., with more than 5 million guest rooms[xvi].

Pros: 24/7 access for both guests and staff. High demand for snacks, especially in the evening and overnight hours.

Cons: High competition from existing food services within the hotel, such as room service or onsite restaurants.

Identification: Focus on hotels with high occupancy rates, particularly those that cater to business travelers or tourists. Check platforms like TripAdvisor, Booking.com, and Hotels.com for reviews and ratings of hotels in your city. Look for hotels with consistently high occupancy rates and positive feedback from guests. You should also visit the websites of individual hotels to find information about their occupancy rates, room availability, and guest reviews. Many hotels publish their average occupancy rates or provide information about peak seasons.

Gyms

Gyms attract fitness enthusiasts looking for healthy snacks and hydration options before or after workouts. Vending machines stocked with sports drinks, protein bars, and healthy snacks cater to this health-conscious audience. The International Health, Racquet & Sportsclub

Association states there are over 40,000 health clubs in the U.S., serving over 71.5 million members[xvii].

Pros: Health-conscious clientele looking for quick, healthy snacks. Consistent traffic throughout the day, particularly before and after work hours.

Cons: Limited to the gym's members, which can restrict the customer base.

Identification: Look for large gyms with a substantial membership base. For me, I like to check the social media pages of local gyms to assess their popularity and membership base. I look for engagement metrics like followers, likes, and comments. The higher the followers and engagement, the better! You should also connect with fitness enthusiasts or personal trainers in your city to get recommendations for popular gyms in the area.

Schools and Dorms

Schools have a large captive audience of students, teachers, and staff who need quick snacks and drinks throughout the day. Vending machines in schools provide convenient options for a busy student population. Research.com reports that there are approximately 130,930 K-12 schools in the U.S., with over 56 million students enrolled[xviii].

College dormitories house students who often require snacks and drinks during late study sessions or on weekends. Vending machines in dormitories cater to the unique schedules and needs of college students. According to Statista.com, Over 20 million students are enrolled in U.S. colleges and universities, many of whom live in campus dormitories[xix].

Pros: Captive audience of students with regular meal schedules. High demand for affordable snacks and drinks.

Cons: Strict regulations regarding product offerings, particularly in K-12 schools.

Identification: Focus on large school districts or college campuses with high enrollment numbers. Research the education department in your country or city for information on school districts and enrollment numbers. You should also visit the websites of local school districts to find information about their size and student population. In the US, The National Center for Education Statistics and college directories can provide valuable data.

Retail Stores

Retail stores see steady customer traffic, making them ideal locations for vending machines. Shoppers often look for quick refreshment options during their shopping experience. According to the National Retail Federation, U.S. retail sales reached over $4 trillion in 2021, with millions of daily shoppers across various retail environments[xx].

Pros: Constant flow of customers throughout the day, especially in large stores or malls. Opportunity to target impulse buyers.

Cons: High competition from other food and beverage outlets within the store or mall.

Identification: Target large retail chains with high customer traffic. Retail industry reports and mall directories can provide foot traffic statistics. A quick internet search can provide you with the information you need.

Gas Stations

Gas stations are frequented by travelers and commuters who appreciate the convenience of vending machines for quick snacks and drinks. These locations operate around the clock, catering to different customer needs. Fueleconomy.gov reported that there are 168,000 gas stations nationwide, serving millions of customers daily[xxi]

Pros: High turnover of customers, particularly during peak travel times. 24/7 access to a steady stream of potential buyers.

Cons: Potentially high competition from the convenience store itself, which may offer similar products.

Identification: Focus on busy gas stations located on major highways or in densely populated areas.

Shopping Centers

Shopping centers and malls attract high foot traffic from shoppers, creating a lucrative opportunity for vending machines. These locations benefit from extended hours and a diverse customer base. According to Worldmetrics.org, there are approximately 1,170 shopping malls in the US. These malls host over 220 million visitors per year[xxii].

Pros: High foot traffic from shoppers, especially on weekends and holidays. Extended hours can lead to increased sales opportunities.

Cons: High rent or revenue-sharing demands, particularly in prime retail spaces.

Identification: Focus on high-traffic malls or shopping centers in affluent areas. Research online directories or real estate listings that specialize in commercial properties. Look for malls and shopping centers located in upscale neighborhoods.

Amusement Parks

Amusement parks have a large influx of visitors seeking refreshments while enjoying the attractions. Vending machines provide a convenient option for guests in high-demand locations. According to Statista.com, Central Park in New York City reigned supreme as the most visited park in 2023, with a staggering 42 million visitors throughout the year.

That's a significant lead over the runner-up, Golden Gate Park in San Francisco, which attracted nearly half the number of visitors, 24 million[xxiii].

Pros: High volume of visitors seeking refreshments while enjoying attractions. Strong demand during peak seasons.

Cons: Highly seasonal, with potential for lower sales during off-peak times.

Identification: Focus on large, popular amusement parks with substantial visitor numbers. Research online travel guides and websites that specialize in attractions. They often list popular amusement parks and provide visitor reviews. Amusement park industry reports for your city can also provide insights into visitor statistics.

Conference Centers

Conference centers host events and meetings, attracting attendees who require quick snack and beverage options between sessions. Vending machines offer convenience and accessibility in these bustling environments. Conference centers can host thousands of visitors per event, with multiple events occurring throughout the year.

Pros: Large groups of attendees in need of quick snacks and beverages between sessions. Regular events mean consistent traffic.

Cons: Traffic is event-dependent, with potential for quiet periods between conferences.

Identification: Target large conference centers in major cities that host multiple events throughout the year. Websites like Eventbrite or Meetup often list conference centers and venues for events. Event calendars and venue directories can provide useful information.

Car Washes

Car washes see regular customer traffic, offering a chance for vending machines to cater to people waiting for their vehicles. Snacks and drinks can enhance the customer experience while they wait. There are about 60,000 carwash locations in the US in 2022, according to Carwash.com. The average car wash location serves approximately 20,000 cars annually[xxiv].

Pros: Regular customer turnover, with customers often waiting for extended periods. Limited competition from other food services.

Cons: Foot traffic is entirely dependent on car wash volume, which can fluctuate.

Identification: Focus on large, well-trafficked car washes, particularly those offering full-service options. Local business directories and industry reports can provide insights.

Concert Venues

Concert venues have high-volume foot traffic during events, with attendees seeking refreshments. Vending machines placed in these venues can capture the demand for quick snacks and drinks. Live Nation, a leading concert promoter, reported hosting over 40,000 events in 2019, drawing millions of attendees (Live Nation, 2019).[xxv]

Pros: Concert venues attract large crowds, creating a captive audience for your vending machines. Also, the excitement and energy of a concert can encourage attendees to make impulse purchases.

Cons: Sales can fluctuate depending on the popularity of the event and the size of the crowd. Some concert venues may have existing food and beverage vendors, potentially limiting your market share.

Identification: Focus on large, popular concert venues in your city or tourist destinations. Check online directories like Ticketmaster to find concert venues in your area. Also, research venue capacity and event schedules to assess potential foot traffic.

Night Clubs

Nightclubs have a steady flow of patrons looking for snacks and drinks to complement their night out. Vending machines can provide after-hours options when other services may not be available. According to IBISWorld, there are 67,531 Bars & Nightclubs businesses in the US as of 2023. The U.S. nightclub industry generates over $2 billion annually, with millions of patrons visiting clubs each year[xxvi].

Pros: Nightclubs often stay open late, allowing your machines to generate revenue beyond traditional business hours. Vending machines can offer snacks and drinks to complement the alcoholic beverages served by nightclubs.

Cons: Some nightclubs may have their own bars, which could limit the demand for vending machines. Also, Nightclubs can be susceptible to damage or theft, requiring additional security measures for your vending machines.

Identification: Look for nightclubs with a reputation for attracting large crowds and a vibrant atmosphere. Nightclubs located in busy entertainment districts or near tourist attractions are more likely to have high foot traffic.

Negotiating Location Agreements

Once you've identified a potential location, the next step is negotiating a fair agreement with the property owner or manager. A well-negotiated contract ensures both parties benefit and sets the groundwork for a successful partnership.

I remember when I first approached the owner of a local gym about placing a vending machine there. I was a bit skeptical and apprehensive at first because there was already a vending machine close to the facility. However, I summoned the courage to proceed when I realized that the other machine didn't offer healthy snacks and drinks, which would perfectly cater to the gym's health-conscious clientele.

When I met with the gym owner, I said, "I understand you already have a vending machine nearby, but I've noticed it lacks healthier options that your members might appreciate. I believe my machine can fill this gap."

The owner nodded thoughtfully and replied, "That's a good point. Our members are always looking for convenient, healthy snacks."

I emphasized how the vending machines would enhance convenience for their visitors and employees. Highlighting these benefits helped me negotiate favorable terms. We eventually came to an agreement where I would pay 20% of my revenue each month. The owner agreed, saying, "If your machine can offer what our members are looking for, I think it will be a great addition."

Building a good relationship was crucial in this process, as it paved the way for a successful partnership that benefitted both parties. Here are some tips for negotiating location agreements:

Understand the Property Owner's Needs: Knowing what the property owner values can help you tailor your pitch. Some might prioritize the additional revenue, while others may focus on providing convenience for their customers or employees. Here's how you can connect with property owners and tailor your pitch to align with their priorities:

Building the Connection

Networking and Introductions:

Start by reaching out to property owners through mutual contacts or professional networks. Attending local business events, joining industry groups, or even using platforms like LinkedIn can help you make initial connections.

Cold Outreach:

If networking doesn't yield results, don't hesitate to reach out directly. A well-crafted email or phone call can open doors, especially if you highlight the mutual benefits of the partnership.

Here's an email format:

Subject: Vending Machine Partnership Opportunity

Dear [Gym Owner's Name],

I hope this email finds you well.

My name is [Your Name], and I'm the owner of [Your Business Name]. I'm reaching out to inquire about a potential vending machine partnership for your gym, [Gym Name].

I believe that a vending machine could be a valuable addition to your gym, offering convenience and additional revenue for your facility. By providing healthy snacks, drinks, and energy bars, we can cater to the needs of your members and enhance their overall gym experience.

I'm confident that a vending machine would be a mutually beneficial partnership. We can discuss terms such as commission rates, machine placement, and product selection to ensure that it aligns with your gym's goals.

I would appreciate the opportunity to discuss this further and answer any questions you may have. Please feel free to contact me at [Your Phone Number] or [Your Email Address].

Thank you for your time and consideration.

Sincerely,

[Your Name]

[Your Business Name]

Key Questions to Ask

When meeting with property owners, ask questions that reveal their priorities:

"What are your goals for this space?" Understanding whether they prioritize revenue, convenience for customers, or enhancing their property can guide your pitch.

"What challenges do you face with your current amenities?" Identifying pain points allows you to position your vending machine as a solution.

"How do your customers or employees currently use this area?" This helps you tailor your product offerings to meet the needs of the people who frequent the space.

Revenue Sharing: Offer a fair commission based on a percentage of the sales. Typically, commissions range from 5% to 20%, depending on the location and traffic. In my experience, I have negotiated terms where I pay as low as 5% each month, which has been beneficial for both my business and the location owners. On the other hand, 20% has been my highest commission so far, as was the case with the gym. It's important to find a balance that works for both parties while considering the potential foot traffic and sales volume at each location. Here are some revenue sharing types you should consider, along with their own sets of pros and cons:

Flat Fee

A flat fee refers to a predetermined, fixed amount that a location owner receives from the vending machine operator, regardless of the total sales generated by the vending machine. Unlike a percentage-based revenue share, where the payout varies based on the machine's earnings, the flat fee remains constant, providing the location owner with a guaranteed payment regardless of performance.

Pros:

Predictable Costs: You pay a set amount, making it easier to budget.

Full Profit Retention: After the flat fee, all sales revenue is yours to keep.

Cons:

Higher Risk: If sales are low, you still owe the fee, which can lead to losses.

Less Incentive for Property Owners: Without a revenue share, property owners might be less motivated to support your vending machine's success.

Things to Consider:

A flat fee works best in locations with consistent, high foot traffic where sales are predictable. Ensure you thoroughly assess the location's potential before committing to a flat fee.

Threshold-Based Hybrid Agreements

Hybrid agreements are arrangements that combine elements of both percentage-based revenue sharing and flat fee payments. In a threshold-based hybrid agreement, the location owner receives a flat fee unless the vending machine's sales or profits fall below a predetermined amount within a specific period. If this threshold isn't met, the owner is paid a percentage of the sales instead of the flat fee.

Example:

A location owner is guaranteed a flat fee of $50 per month. However, if the vending machine's sales or profits don't reach $600 in any given month, the owner receives 10% of the profit instead. For instance, if sales amount to $400 in a month, the owner would receive $40 (10% of $400) instead of the $50 flat fee. If sales are $600 or more, the owner only receives the $50 flat fee.

Pros:

Balanced Risk: The threshold-based structure provides a predictable income for the location owner while also allowing flexibility if sales fall below expectations.

Incentive for Higher Sales: The location owner has a vested interest in driving sales, as they benefit from higher percentages if the threshold isn't met.

Cons:

Complex Negotiations: Establishing the right threshold and percentage can be challenging, requiring careful negotiation to satisfy both parties.

Things to Consider:

Hybrid agreements, where a flat fee is combined with a conditional percentage of sales, work best in situations where there's high potential but some unpredictability. They offer a safety net for location owners while encouraging them to actively contribute to your vending machine's success. This setup is particularly useful in markets where both parties want to share the risks and rewards more evenly.

Contract Duration: Discuss and agree on the contract's length. Short-term contracts offer flexibility, while long-term agreements provide stability. For instance, if you're unsure how well your products will sell at a new office building, a six-month contract gives you the opportunity to evaluate sales and customer preferences without a long-term commitment.

On the other hand, long-term agreements provide stability and can be beneficial for high-performing locations. For example, after successfully running a vending machine in a busy hospital for a year, you might negotiate a two-year contract to ensure continued access to the high foot traffic and steady sales. This long-term commitment can also strengthen your relationship with the property owner, potentially leading to better terms and opportunities in the future.

Exclusivity Clause: To protect your business, negotiate an exclusivity clause that prevents competitors from placing similar machines nearby. This may sound brutal, but it's just business. Exclusivity can give you an edge by reducing competition and increasing sales opportunities.

I learned about the importance of exclusivity the hard way. When I approached a hotel manager in Atlanta about placing a vending machine in their lobby, his response was unexpectedly negative. The conversation left me puzzled, and I briefly suspected he might own the existing machine in the facility.

Later, an old friend who works at the hotel called to tell me that the real owner of the machine had negotiated an exclusivity clause. While the news was frustrating, I could understand the strategy behind it. As a business person, I respect the tactic because it ensures the machine's success in that location by eliminating direct competition.

Legal Considerations and Permits

Running a vending machine business involves understanding and complying with various legal requirements and regulations. This ensures smooth operations and avoids potential legal issues.

Permits and Licenses: Depending on your location, you may need permits or licenses to operate vending machines. For instance, in Atlanta, I had to apply for a business license and a vending machine permit. The cost and process can vary, so it's important to check with local government offices or business bureaus.

Where to Get Information:

Start by visiting your city or county's official website. Look for the business licensing or permits section, where you can find information specific to vending machines. Local chambers of commerce or small business development centers are also valuable resources.

Typical Requirements:

You may need a general business license, a vending machine permit, and possibly health department approval if you're selling food or beverages. Requirements often include submitting an application, paying fees, and passing inspections.

Typical Fees:

Fees vary widely but can range from $50 to $300 per machine annually, depending on your location. In some cities, you may also need to renew your license yearly.

Health and Safety Regulations: Ensure your machines meet health and safety standards, especially if you're offering food or beverages. Regular maintenance and cleanliness are essential to comply with regulations and to maintain customer trust.

Compliance Tips:

Regular Maintenance: Ensure your machines are clean, well-stocked, and functioning properly.

Food Safety: If you sell perishable items, comply with health department guidelines on refrigeration and expiration dates.

Labeling: Assuming you have homemade products that have been certified by the relevant organizations in your state or country, ensure that you display nutritional information and ingredient lists clearly.

Where to Find Regulations:

The U.S. Food and Drug Administration (FDA) provides guidelines for vending machine operations, particularly for food safety. Your state or country's health department website will have additional local regulations.

Insurance: Protect your investment by obtaining liability insurance. This covers potential damages or accidents related to your machines.

Types of Insurance Coverage:

General Liability Insurance: Protects your business against claims of bodily injury, property damage, and personal injury related to your vending machines. For instance, if a customer gets injured while using your machine, this insurance can cover legal fees and any settlements.

Product Liability Insurance: Covers claims related to the products you sell, such as food poisoning or allergic reactions. This is especially important if you sell perishable goods.

Property Insurance: Protects your vending machines against damage or loss due to events like theft, vandalism, or natural disasters. Some policies also cover the cost of repairs or replacement.

Business Interruption Insurance: If a covered event forces you to halt operations temporarily, this insurance can help cover lost income and ongoing expenses.

Choosing the Right Coverage:

When selecting insurance, consider the locations of your machines, the products you sell, and the specific risks associated with your business. Consulting with an insurance broker who specializes in small businesses can help you find a policy that fits your needs. A quick online search for brokers in your city will connect you to reputable agencies.

Cost Considerations:

Insurance premiums vary based on factors such as the value of your machines, the types of products you sell, and the locations of your machines. On average, expect to pay between $400 and $1,000 annually per machine for comprehensive coverage.

Legal Requirements:

In some areas, certain types of insurance may be mandatory, especially if you're placing machines in public spaces or government buildings. Check with local authorities to ensure compliance with any insurance regulations.

In summary, finding and securing the right locations involves a mix of strategic planning, effective negotiation, and adherence to legal requirements. With careful consideration and the right approach, you can maximize your vending machine business's potential and build a successful operation.

Up next: We will explore strategies for selecting and managing your inventory. From building relationships with suppliers to implementing efficient restocking schedules, you will learn everything you need to know to create a winning product mix.

CHAPTER 6:
Stocking Your Vending Machines

Choosing the right products for your vending machines is essential for maximizing profits. The products you offer should cater to the needs and preferences of your target customers. Start by considering the location of your machine. For example, if your machine is in a gym or fitness center, stocking it with healthy snacks like protein bars, bottled water, and sports drinks would be a smart choice. On the other hand, a machine in an office building might do well with a mix of snacks, beverages, and even some healthier options for the health-conscious.

I learned this the hard way when I made a costly mistake with one of my vending machines. A friend of mine, Marcus, lived in an apartment complex in Atlanta. Marcus was vegan and had met a few other vegans in his building. From these encounters, he concluded that 90% of the residents were vegan. Excited by the prospect of tapping into a niche market, I didn't bother to ask how he knew or do any research of my own. I just decided to go all in. The next month, I placed a vending machine in that complex and stocked it exclusively with vegan products.

Well, all I can say is that it was a disaster! For almost five weeks, only four packets of kale chips were sold, despite all the marketing I did for the machine and the products. I have a sneaking suspicion that it was Marcus who bought those four packets, trying to help me out, but who knows? I was frustrated and angry, not knowing what to think until it struck me: I never actually researched my target audience. I had blindly believed the statistics Marcus gave me.

One evening, determined to figure out what was going wrong, I decided to observe the machine closely and maybe meet a few residents. Luckily, I struck up a conversation with a lady hanging around the machine area. After chatting for a few minutes, she mentioned she could really use a snack. I eagerly pointed to the vending machine and told her to help herself. Her response was a mild shock: “I’m not vegan!” I swore under my breath, feeling my frustration boil over. I asked her, "But isn’t everyone who lives here vegan?” She looked at me with wide eyes and asked, “And how did you come about that assumption?”

I quickly explained that it was Marcus, my friend who lived there, who told me that. She shook her head, saying, “Well, your friend is wrong. Most of us aren’t vegan.”

To rectify this blunder, I quickly put out a survey to learn more about the residents’ preferences. I even offered incentives to encourage participation. The results were eye-opening. It turned out that only 10% of the residents were vegan. A whopping 80% were meat eaters, and the remaining 10% were flexitarian.

With this new information, I restocked the machine with a diverse selection of products that appealed to all three groups. Sales picked up almost immediately, and I was able to turn the situation around. This experience taught me a valuable lesson: always do your homework before stocking your vending machines. Don’t rely on assumptions, even if they come from well-meaning friends.

So, you see that understanding your customer base is key. Now, if your machine is placed in a school, you might want to avoid stocking it with too many sugary snacks. Instead, consider options like granola bars, fruit snacks, and juice boxes. In contrast, a machine at a bus station might benefit from quick, energy-boosting items like candy bars, chips, and sodas. Always keep in mind who will be using your machine and what they might be looking for during their day.

However, it's also wise to offer a variety of products to cater to different tastes and dietary needs, like I later did with the machine at the apartment complex. Consider including gluten-free, vegan, or low-sugar options alongside more traditional snacks. This not only broadens your customer base but also shows that you're considerate of different needs.

Establishing Relationships with Suppliers

Finding reliable suppliers is just as important as selecting the right products. A good supplier can make all the difference in keeping your machines well-stocked with high-quality items. To begin, research suppliers who specialize in vending machine products. Start by performing a simple online search using terms like *"vending machine product suppliers in [YOUR CITY]"* or *"wholesale snack suppliers in [YOUR CITY]."* You can also check industry directories or online forums where vending machine operators discuss their experiences. Attending trade shows or industry events is another valuable resource where you can meet suppliers face-to-face and learn more about their offerings.

To find out about upcoming trade shows and industry events, you can start by researching online. Websites like Eventbrite.com,

ExpoFP.com, and even social media platforms often list industry-specific events. You can also subscribe to newsletters from vending industry associations or magazines, which frequently announce such events. Additionally, networking with other vending machine operators can be a great way to hear about events that may not be widely advertised.

Another practical approach is joining vending machine forums or online communities where industry professionals discuss upcoming trade shows and events. These forums can also provide valuable insights into which events are worth attending based on your specific needs, whether you're looking for suppliers, learning opportunities, or networking.

When you attend a trade show, it's important to make the most of the opportunity to meet suppliers face-to-face. Start by preparing a list of questions to ask each supplier. This might include questions about their product range, pricing, delivery times, and any special terms they might offer for bulk purchases.

When you approach a supplier, introduce yourself and briefly explain your business and what you're looking for. For example, you might say, "Hi, I'm Russell, and I operate several vending machines across different locations. I'm looking for reliable suppliers who can provide quality snacks and beverages. Can you tell me more about what you offer and how you work with businesses like mine?"

Be sure to listen carefully to their responses and take notes on what stands out. It's also helpful to ask for samples or brochures that you can review later. If a supplier seems like a good fit, don't hesitate to ask about any trade show specials or discounts they might be offering. These events are often a great time to negotiate favorable terms, especially if you're considering a large order.

Supplier Relationships in Practice

When I first started in the vending machine business, I was fortunate to find a great supplier right off the bat. John came highly recommended by another business owner, who was kind enough to link us up. This connection was a game-changer for my business. John was not just reliable but also deeply knowledgeable about the industry. He was the first supplier I worked with, and as my business grew, I started engaging in the services of other suppliers to meet the demands of my machines in different locations. However, John remains one of my go-to suppliers, especially for high-demand products.

John operates in a straightforward yet highly efficient manner. We began by discussing my initial needs—everything from snacks and drinks to specialized items that catered to specific locations. He provided me with a catalog, which included a range of products along with their wholesale prices. We then discussed delivery schedules, and he was flexible enough to accommodate my restocking needs, which vary depending on the machine's location. John's flexibility, reliability, and ability to supply fresh products consistently have helped my business maintain a steady flow of satisfied customers. Our relationship has grown stronger over time, and it's this kind of partnership that has been instrumental in my success.

Building a strong relationship with your suppliers is key to long-term success. Regular communication is important—keep them informed about your business needs, and be open to their suggestions as well. I make it a point to check in with John and other suppliers regularly, not just to place orders but to discuss trends in the market, upcoming product launches, or even just to catch up. This ongoing dialogue has led to better pricing, priority service, and access to exclusive products that my competitors don't have.

You should also consider working with multiple suppliers. This approach ensures that you have a backup plan if one supplier is unable to deliver on time or if a product becomes unavailable. Having multiple sources for your products helps you maintain consistency in stocking your machines, which in turn keeps your customers happy.

For anyone starting out, once you've identified potential suppliers, reach out to them directly. You can call them, send an email, or even set up a meeting if they are local. During your initial contact, discuss the products they offer, the pricing structure, and the delivery schedules. When discussing pricing, don't just settle for the first quote they give you. Ask about discounts for bulk purchases or any promotions they might be running. For example, I once negotiated a 10% discount on a large order by agreeing to a slightly longer delivery window, which helped me save money without affecting my operations.

When it comes to product offerings, ask for samples. Suppliers are usually more than willing to send samples of their products so you can test them out before making a larger commitment. This also gives you a chance to evaluate the quality of the items they'll be providing. Discuss their delivery schedules in detail—find out how frequently they can deliver, whether they can handle urgent requests, and what their minimum order requirements are. Make sure to negotiate terms that work for both you and the supplier. In my case, I’ve arranged for bi-weekly deliveries for some machines and weekly deliveries for others based on the volume of sales.

Top Suppliers I Work with in Atlanta

Over time, I've developed relationships with a number of suppliers, but there are a few that stand out as my top go-to sources in Atlanta:

- **ACC Wholesale:** They specialize in wholesale distribution of candy, snacks, juices, sodas, sports drinks, and sundries. ACC Wholesale has been a reliable partner, providing me with the essential products that keep my machines stocked with popular items. Their prompt deliveries and competitive pricing make them a crucial part of my supply chain.

- **Campbell's Foodservice:** Campbell's supplies me with premium soups, craveable eats, treats, snacks, and beverage brands that consumers love. Their products are especially popular in locations where customers are looking for a mix of quality and convenience.
- **Redstone Foods:** Redstone Foods offers an extensive range of bulk candy, novelty candy, old-fashioned candy, and fine chocolates. Their selection is perfect for catering to customers with a sweet tooth, and they've helped me diversify my product offerings to attract a broader customer base.
- **Back to Nature:** They provide me with all plant-based products, including cookies, crackers, granola, nuts, and trail mix. Back to Nature's products are a hit in locations where customers are health-conscious or have dietary restrictions. Their range of gluten-free and vegan options has helped me meet the growing demand for healthier snack choices.

Currently, I work with 17 different suppliers to stock my fleet of 50 vending machines. Each supplier has a specific role—some provide general snacks and drinks, while others specialize in niche products that cater to particular locations. For instance, I have a supplier who exclusively provides healthy snacks for my machines in gyms and fitness centers. For specialty items like organic snacks or gluten-free options, I rely on smaller, niche suppliers like Back to Nature. By diversifying my supplier base, I've been able to ensure that my machines are always stocked. Also, with the balance between large-scale suppliers and specialized providers, I can cater to a wider range of customer preferences.

Operating with multiple suppliers might sound complicated, but it's all about organization and clear communication. I have a schedule that I stick to for placing orders, and I use inventory management software (VendSoft) to keep track of stock levels and reorder points. This way, I can ensure that all my machines are well-stocked without over-ordering or running out of products. Additionally, I maintain a good relationship with each supplier by being upfront about my needs, paying invoices on time, and keeping an open line of communication.

Working with multiple suppliers will not only help you maintain consistency but also give you the flexibility to offer a wide range of products tailored to different customer preferences. This strategy has been a cornerstone of my business success and has kept my customers coming back for more.

Managing Inventory and Restocking Schedules

Once your machines are stocked with the right products from reliable suppliers, the next step is managing your inventory effectively. Proper inventory management is essential to ensure that your vending machines remain stocked with the products your customers want, and it helps you avoid the pitfalls of overstocking or running out of popular items.

Practical Ways to Manage Inventory

One of the most practical ways to manage your inventory is to implement a systematic approach to tracking what goes into and out of your machines. Start by creating an inventory log for each machine. This log should include details such as the product name, quantity stocked, date of restocking, and any notes on sales trends. You can use a simple spreadsheet to track this information. For example, in my early days, when I had about three machines, I relied heavily on a detailed spreadsheet that I updated every time I visited a machine. I would record how many of each product I had added and then note down the remaining inventory during my next visit.

Another practical tip is to categorize your products by type or by popularity. For instance, you can group snacks, beverages, and specialty items separately in your inventory log. This helps you quickly identify which category needs more frequent restocking. As your business grows, you may want to upgrade from a spreadsheet to inventory management software, like VendSoft or VendSys, which can automate much of this process.

Tracking What Sells and What Doesn’t

Keeping track of what sells and what doesn’t is crucial to maintaining a successful vending operation. When I first started, I manually reviewed my sales logs, comparing inventory sheets to the quantities stocked. While this method worked, it was time-consuming and left room for human error. Fortunately, inventory management software has streamlined this process, automatically tracking sales and generating reports that highlight what’s performing well and what isn’t.

To effectively monitor sales, start by creating a simple sales tracking sheet if you're not using software. Record the product name, the number of items sold, and any observable patterns. For instance, you might notice that certain products sell out quickly during the first week of the month but slow down afterward. Recognizing these patterns allows you to adjust your stocking strategy to meet demand more accurately.

Another key factor to consider is the placement of products inside the vending machine. You've probably heard the phrase, "Eye level is buy level." Studies have shown that items placed at eye level are more likely to be chosen by customers. This means that high-demand products should be positioned where they are easily visible and accessible. If a product isn't selling as well as expected, it could be due to its location in the machine rather than a lack of interest. Rearranging the layout by placing popular or promotional items at eye level can potentially boost their sales.

In my experience, products that didn't sell well often ended up taking up valuable space in my machines, which could have been better utilized by more popular items. To address this, I began conducting monthly reviews of my sales data, identifying slow movers, and replacing them with new or different products. If a particular item wasn't selling after two months, I would swap it out and try something else based on customer feedback or trends I observed in other locations.

Monitoring Sales Data

Monitoring sales data is one of the most effective ways to stay on top of your inventory. The first step is to establish a routine for checking your sales data. This could be weekly, bi-weekly, or monthly, depending on the traffic your machines receive. When I first started, I made it a habit to check my sales logs at the end of every week. This helped me identify which products were consistently popular and which ones were underperforming.

As my business grew, I transitioned to using a software, VendSoft, which allowed me to monitor sales data in real-time. With this software, I could see exactly what was selling in each machine at any given moment. The ability to monitor sales data in real-time was a game-changer for me. It allowed me to react quickly to trends, such as increasing the stock of a popular item before it sold out or phasing out a product that wasn't performing well.

Before I started using inventory management software, I often found myself either overstocking or understocking my machines. This was mainly because I was relying on rough estimates and periodic checks. For instance, there were times when I would visit a machine only to find that a top-selling product had been sold out for days, which meant I had missed out on potential sales. Other times, I would overstock certain items, leading to wasted inventory, especially for perishable goods.

After I implemented the software, managing inventory became much more streamlined. The software tracked every sale automatically and provided me with reports that I could review at any time. This meant that I no longer had to manually check each machine's stock levels or guess which products were performing well. Instead, I could make informed decisions based on accurate, real-time data. This shift not only saved me time but also significantly improved my profitability.

Creating a Restocking Schedule

A well-planned restocking schedule is vital for keeping your vending machines running smoothly. To create an effective restocking schedule, start by analyzing the sales volume and traffic patterns for each machine. Machines located in high-traffic areas, such as busy office buildings or schools, may require more frequent restocking, perhaps even multiple times a week. On the other hand, machines in quieter locations might only need to be restocked once every two weeks.

For example, one of my machines located in a high-traffic office building sees a lot of sales during the workweek but slows down over the weekend. To ensure it stays stocked, I set up a schedule to restock it every Monday and Thursday. In contrast, another machine I have in a smaller office only needs to be checked and restocked once a week, usually on Fridays.

When setting up your restocking schedule, it's important to coordinate with your suppliers. If you're working with multiple suppliers, you'll need to make sure their delivery schedules align with your restocking needs. For example, I coordinate with John, my go-to supplier, to have deliveries of high-demand items every Monday morning so I can restock my busiest machines first thing in the week. For my other suppliers, I've arranged deliveries on specific days that match up with my planned visits to those machines.

Using Inventory Management Software

Inventory management software has been one of the most valuable tools in managing my vending business. Before I started using it, I faced numerous challenges, such as missed restocking opportunities, overstocking, and the inefficiency of manually tracking sales. These issues soon became a thing of the past when I implemented VendSoft.

VendSoft tracks sales and inventory levels automatically, giving me a clear picture of what's happening with each machine at any given time. I can easily access this information from my phone and tablet, which means I can monitor my business even when I'm not on-site. The software sends me alerts when a product is running low or when a machine hasn't made a sale in a while, indicating a possible issue that needs my attention.

Before using VendSoft, I relied on periodic checks, which sometimes led to stockouts or surplus inventory. Now, I can set automatic reorder points for each product. When stock reaches a certain level, VendSoft notifies me, allowing me to reorder in time to avoid running out. This has helped me maintain a consistent supply and reduce waste from overordering.

In addition to tracking inventory, VendSoft assists in planning restocking schedules. It provides data on peak sales times, which I use to optimize my restocking visits. For example, if the data shows that sales are highest in the middle of the week, I'll schedule my visits around that time to ensure the machines are fully stocked when demand is greatest.

Overall, the transition to using VendSoft has drastically improved the efficiency of my operations. It has allowed me to focus more on growing the business rather than spending hours on manual inventory checks and data entry. I highly recommend investing in this type of software as soon as your business starts to grow, as it will save you time, reduce errors, and ultimately increase your profits.

There are also other great inventory management software options out there, like Zoho Inventory, known for its ease of use and integration with other business tools, and Vendsys, which offers comprehensive vending management solutions, including route management and financial reporting. Each of these options has unique features, so it's worth exploring which one best fits your business needs. Investing in inventory management software early on can save you time, reduce errors, and ultimately increase your profits.

In summary, stocking your vending machines involves thoughtful product selection, building strong relationships with suppliers, and efficiently managing inventory. Each of these elements contributes to the overall success of your vending machine business. By paying attention to the details and staying organized, you can ensure that your machines are always ready to meet the needs of your customers.

Up next: Properly maintaining your vending machines is crucial for ensuring their longevity, preventing breakdowns, and maintaining customer satisfaction. The next chapter will guide you through essential maintenance tasks, common troubleshooting steps, and security measures to protect your investment.

CHAPTER 7:
Maintenance and Troubleshooting

Maintenance and troubleshooting are important in any business. Whether it's a small coffee shop, a delivery service, or a vending machine operation, keeping things in good shape can make all the difference. Regular upkeep helps catch minor issues before they turn into big problems. It saves money in the long run and keeps customers happy. This is especially true for vending machines, where a broken or malfunctioning unit can lead to lost sales, frustrated customers, and costly repairs. I learned this lesson early on in my vending machine business.

When I first started, I thought that since the machines were new, they didn't need much attention. I assumed they would just keep working without a hitch. But I quickly realized that wasn't the case. Vending machines, whether new or old, need regular care. New machines might have fewer problems, but they still need routine checks to make sure everything is working correctly. Sensors can get dirty, coils can shift, and software can glitch. With older machines, regular maintenance becomes even more important, as parts wear out more quickly and need to be replaced or adjusted more often. I found that new machines require at least a monthly check, while older ones might need more frequent attention, sometimes every week.

In my early days of running vending machines, I had only two machines to look after. I had no choice but to learn how to do basic maintenance and troubleshooting on my own. I remember one of my first lessons clearly: I skipped a regular check-up, thinking everything was fine because the machine was still new. A week later, I got a call from a customer saying that a snack was stuck in the machine. When I arrived, I discovered a small piece of debris had jammed the mechanism. It was a simple fix, but it taught me the value of regular upkeep. I made it a habit to clean the coin and bill acceptors weekly, restock items carefully, and check for expired products.

I also learned to test the machine's sensors and motors to make sure everything was functioning correctly. I began wiping down the glass and keypad regularly, not just for cleanliness but also to make the machine more appealing to customers. These small tasks became part of my routine, helping to prevent more serious issues down the road. At the time, it felt like a lot to handle, but I knew that being proactive was better than dealing with a breakdown.

As my business grew and I added more machines to my fleet, I realized I couldn't handle everything myself. I had more locations, different types of machines, and new challenges. I started engaging professionals for the more technical stuff, like software updates, complex repairs, or when the refrigeration unit on a machine started acting up. The professionals taught me a lot, but I still kept doing the basic maintenance myself. This balance allowed me to keep costs down and focus on expanding the business, knowing that my machines were in good hands.

As a business person, you must always find ways to save costs whenever possible. Every penny saved on maintenance or repairs can go back into growing your business. But it's important to be smart about where you cut costs. Saving money should never come at the expense of the health of your business or the satisfaction of your customers. That's why learning basic maintenance and troubleshooting for your vending machines is so valuable.

Common Issues and How to Fix Them

In my experience running vending machines, I've come across a number of common problems. Some were simple and easy to fix, while others required a bit more time and patience. But I learned that with a little know-how and some practice, many of these issues could be resolved without needing to call a professional. I got lucky in the beginning because the businesses I bought my machines from usually gave me a thorough tutorial on potential problems and how to fix them. They walked me through what to do if a coin jammed, how to reset a frozen machine, and even taught me how to handle minor software glitches. Sometimes, when I faced a problem I wasn’t prepared for, I found myself watching videos online, pausing and replaying them until I got it right. These resources were invaluable and made me realize that most basic problems aren’t too difficult to handle.

Here are some common issues that vending machines might face and the steps I’ve learned to fix them. I’ll start with the simpler problems and move to the more complicated ones.

1. Bill or Coin Jams

Problem: Bills or coins can get stuck in the acceptor, preventing the machine from taking more money. This usually happens when a bill is crumpled, folded, or inserted incorrectly, or if a coin gets caught in the mechanism.

How to Identify: The machine might display an error message, or customers may report that it's not accepting their money. Sometimes, you can hear the acceptor struggling or clicking, which is a sign that something is stuck.

Solution: Open the machine carefully and inspect the bill or coin acceptor. Look for any visible jam. If you see a crumpled bill, gently pull it out without tearing it. For coins, try to locate where they're stuck. Most machines have a small lever or release mechanism for clearing jams. Clean the acceptor's sensors using a soft cloth, as dust and dirt can also cause jams. Regularly check the acceptor for debris and clean it to prevent future problems.

2. Products Not Dispensing Properly

Problem: Sometimes, a product might not drop when a customer makes a selection. This is often due to a misaligned coil or a product getting stuck against the glass.

How to Identify: Customers will report that their product didn't dispense. The machine may show that it's out of stock even when it isn't. You may also notice that products are stuck or look improperly placed.

Solution: Open the machine and check the position of the coils. Realign any that seem bent or out of place. Gently adjust any items that look stuck or improperly loaded. If the problem is recurring, consider replacing the coil or moving heavier products to slots with stronger motors.

3. Refrigeration Issues

Problem: For machines that offer perishable items, refrigeration problems are common. The machine may not cool properly, causing drinks or snacks to spoil or melt.

How to Identify: The temperature inside the machine feels warmer than it should. Customers may report that their drinks aren't cold. You might also see condensation on the glass or inside the machine.

Solution: Check if the machine is placed near a heat source, like direct sunlight or a warm air vent. If so, move it to a cooler location. Make sure the cooling fan is running, and clean any dust or debris blocking the air vents. If the issue persists, check the thermostat settings and adjust if needed. Sometimes, the compressor might need replacement, which is a more advanced fix requiring professional help.

4. Display or Screen Malfunctions

Problem: The display screen may not show the correct information, or it could be blank, preventing customers from making selections.

How to Identify: The screen is blank, flickering, or showing incorrect or garbled text. Customers might report difficulty using the machine.

Solution: Start by checking the power connections to the display. Ensure all cables are properly connected and there's no visible damage. Sometimes, a simple restart of the machine can fix minor software glitches. If the screen is cracked or damaged, it may need to be replaced, which can be done by following the machine's manual or calling a technician.

5. Payment System Failures

Problem: The card reader or contactless payment system might not work, causing frustration for customers who prefer not to use cash.

How to Identify: Customers may complain that their card isn't being read, or you might see an error message on the payment terminal.

Solution: Check the card reader's connection to the machine's main control board. Sometimes, simply cleaning the card reader can solve the problem if it's dirty or dusty. Ensure the machine has a stable internet or network connection, as payment systems often require this to function. Restarting the payment system might also help. If these steps don't solve the problem, contact the manufacturer for technical support or replace the payment terminal.

6. Machine Not Powering On

Problem: The machine does not turn on or loses power intermittently.

How to Identify: The machine appears completely dead, with no lights or sounds, or it might turn on and off sporadically.

Solution: Check the power cord and plug for damage. Ensure it's securely plugged into a working outlet. Check the circuit breaker or fuse box to ensure there isn't a tripped breaker. If there's still no power, the issue might be with the machine's internal power supply, which may require a technician to fix or replace.

7. Software Errors or Glitches

Problem: The machine might display error codes or stop working due to software glitches.

How to Identify: Error codes are displayed on the screen, or the machine stops responding to input.

Solution: Refer to the machine's manual to interpret the error codes. Sometimes, a simple reset can resolve software glitches. Update the machine's software if an update is available. If the problem persists, contact the machine manufacturer or a technician for more specialized support.

8. Machine Vandalism or Tampering

Problem: Machines can be vandalized or tampered with, leading to malfunction or theft.

How to Identify: Look for signs of forced entry, broken locks, or missing products. The machine may also display errors related to cash or stock levels.

Solution: Strengthen security by using more robust locks and consider installing a camera nearby to monitor the machine. Regularly check for signs of tampering and ensure that the machine is placed in a well-lit, secure location.

If you find yourself unsure about how to fix a particular issue, even those listed here as basic, don't hesitate to enlist the help of a technician. While learning to handle simple problems is great for saving time and money, there are times when professional expertise is necessary to avoid causing more damage or risking safety.

Finding a Professional Technician

To find a technician, you can start by contacting the company or dealer from whom you purchased your machine; they often have recommended service professionals. You can also search online for technicians in your area who specialize in vending machine repair. Many local business directories, like Yelp or Google My Business, can provide reviews and ratings to help you choose someone reliable. You may also want to ask other vending machine operators in your area for referrals. Building a relationship with a trusted technician can be very helpful, especially as your business grows and the issues become more complex.

Ensuring Machine Security

Security is essential in any business, whether you're running a small operation or managing a large fleet of vending machines. Businesses that fail to prioritize security often end up facing unnecessary losses, whether it's theft, vandalism, or other damage. For vending machine operators, security should always be a top concern. In the U.S., vending machines are surprisingly frequent targets for theft and vandalism because they are often left unattended for long periods.

I learned the hard way how important security is. It was a Friday night, around 10 p.m., when I got a call from a store manager at one of my busiest locations. My heart sank as he said, "I think your vending machine was broken into." I rushed over, and sure enough, the glass was smashed, and several rows of snacks were gone. The cash box had also been emptied. I felt a mix of anger, frustration, and worry because I realized I hadn't done enough to secure that machine.

I immediately called the police and filed a report. The officers who came to the scene were helpful but warned me that these cases were often hard to solve unless there was clear evidence. Luckily, a nearby security camera managed to capture a partial view of the thief's face as he left the scene. The police had suspicions about who it might be, but without enough evidence, they didn't want to make an arrest just yet.

A few days later, a detective who had been working on the case noticed something unusual while reviewing the footage. The way the thief walked caught his eye—it was distinctive, almost like a limp with a twist. He remembered seeing a similar walk from a suspect in another case. The detective made the connection and shared it with his team. They then reviewed their files and realized that the guy they had suspected initially also had the same walk. This unusual clue convinced the rest of the team that they had their man. The thief was eventually arrested and confessed to breaking into my machine, among others.

The break-in taught me a lot, and I realized I had made a few mistakes that made it easier for the thief to break in. For one, I had placed the machine in a relatively hidden corner of the location, where it wasn't visible from the main entrance. The lock on the cash box was also old and a bit rusty; I hadn't thought to replace it. I quickly learned my lesson and took several steps to ensure my machines would never be easy targets again.

Security Measures to Prevent Theft and Vandalism

Here are the key security measures I now use to protect my machines and that you should consider as well:

Choose Safe Locations: Always place your machines in well-lit, high-traffic areas where potential thieves are less likely to take the risk. Locations near entrances or within sight of staff or security cameras are ideal. Avoid secluded spots or corners.

Install Stronger Locks: Invest in high-quality locks that are resistant to picking, drilling, or cutting. Consider using locks with unique keys that are not easily duplicated. If possible, add a secondary lock mechanism inside the machine to protect the cash box or valuable products.

Use Security Cameras: If possible, install a small, discreet security camera near your machines. Cameras should cover all angles and be in locations that make tampering difficult. Ensure the camera feed is clear and that you regularly check and maintain them to ensure they're working properly.

Regular Inspections: Make a habit of visiting your machines frequently, not just to restock, but to check for signs of tampering or damage. If you see scratches near the lock or any unusual marks, investigate further.

Install Alarms or Anti-Tamper Devices: Some vending machines can be equipped with alarms or sensors that alert you when they're being tampered with or moved. These can be connected to your phone, so you receive immediate notifications. Machines like the Crane Media2 come equipped with built-in alarm systems and tamper sensors that can alert you to any unauthorized access or movement.

Secure the Base: For machines placed outdoors or in public spaces, consider bolting them to the ground or using anti-tip devices to make them harder to move. This reduces the risk of someone trying to tip the machine over or steal it entirely.

Cashless Payment Systems: Transition to card or mobile payments to reduce the amount of cash stored in the machine. This reduces the incentive for thieves to break in, as there's little cash to steal.

Use Tamper-Resistant Glass: If your machines have large glass fronts, consider using shatterproof or tamper-resistant glass. It makes breaking into the machine much harder and deters casual vandals.

Decoy Cash Boxes: You can also use decoy cash boxes that are difficult to reach or require additional steps to access. Thieves might get frustrated and leave without anything of value.

Build Relationships with Nearby Businesses: Establish good relationships with nearby businesses or security personnel. They can help keep an eye on your machine and report any suspicious activity.

Insurance: Make sure your machines are insured against theft and vandalism. This won't prevent a crime, but it can help reduce the financial loss if something does happen.

If you follow these steps, you'll significantly reduce the chances of your machines being targeted by thieves or vandals. But if you're ever unsure about a particular security measure or how to implement it, don't hesitate to consult with a professional security service or your local police department. They often have valuable insights about common crimes in your area and can offer advice tailored to your specific situation.

This chapter covered the essentials of maintaining, troubleshooting, and securing vending machines to keep them running efficiently. Regular maintenance, such as cleaning, checking sensors, and inspecting components, can prevent small issues from becoming major problems. I also shared personal experiences with common issues, like jammed bills and misaligned coils, and provided practical solutions to handle them. As your business grows, it's wise to learn basic repairs while knowing when to bring in professional help.

Security is equally important—protecting your machines with strong locks, security cameras, and alarms can prevent theft and vandalism. Always place machines in well-lit, high-traffic areas and consider cashless payment systems to reduce risk. A proactive approach to both maintenance and security will help you minimize downtime, protect your investment, and keep your business running smoothly.

Up next: Take your vending business to the next level! In the next chapter, we'll dive into the art of marketing your vending machines—because even the best machines need a little promotion to reach their full potential. This chapter is crucial if you are looking to stand out in the market and attract more customers.

CHAPTER 8:
Marketing Your Vending Business

Marketing is the backbone of any successful business. It's the bridge that connects what you offer with the people who need or want it. No matter how great your product or service is, without effective marketing, it can easily get lost in the crowd. Whether you're running a real estate company, an internet marketing agency, or a vending machine business, the right marketing strategies can be the difference between thriving and barely getting by. Marketing isn't just for big brands with massive budgets;

it's essential for businesses of all sizes, including small, local operations like vending machines.

Allow me to share a personal story that not only inspires others but also continues to inspire me. I love to tell it whenever I get the chance. In fact, it's my go-to story—my favorite case study or proof whenever I'm trying to convince a client about the power of marketing their business.

In 2018, I worked with a client who was struggling to make a mark in the crowded market of wellness products. The client's product was called EcoShine, a biodegradable and eco-friendly cleaner made from natural ingredients like citrus extracts and coconut oil. Unlike many other cleaning products, EcoShine was not just environmentally friendly—it was also safe to use around children and pets, which made it a perfect choice for health-conscious families. Despite these great features, the client was feeling overwhelmed. They felt like they were too small to compete with the big names dominating the market, and their sales were flat.

The first thing I did was take a closer look at EcoShine and identify what truly set it apart from the rest. While many brands were shouting about being "green" or "natural," EcoShine had a unique formula that was 100% biodegradable, left no toxic residues, and had an incredibly pleasant citrus scent. We realized that these qualities could appeal not only to eco-conscious consumers but also to parents, pet owners, and people sensitive to chemicals in traditional cleaning products. I knew we had to emphasize these unique selling points to stand out in the market.

Next, we needed to get this message in front of the right audience. I suggested a targeted social media campaign but with a twist. Instead of just posting generic ads, we created engaging content that told the story behind EcoShine. We crafted posts that highlighted real-life scenarios where EcoShine was the hero—like a mom cleaning up after a toddler without worrying about harmful chemicals or a pet owner using it to safely clean their home. We paired these stories with eye-catching visuals, featuring bright, vibrant images of homes and happy families using the product.

We decided to focus primarily on Instagram and Facebook, where a large number of our target audience spent their time. We started by identifying key influencers in the eco-friendly lifestyle space—bloggers, moms, pet lovers, and health enthusiasts—who shared similar values with the brand. We sent them free samples of EcoShine and asked for their honest reviews. Many of them loved the product and began sharing it with their followers. This created authentic buzz and word-of-mouth marketing that felt genuine and trustworthy.

We also ran a series of highly targeted ads. We used Facebook's advanced audience targeting tools to reach users who were interested in green living, parenting, and pet care or had recently engaged with similar brands. We A/B tested different versions of our ads, experimenting with various headlines, images, and calls to action to find the combination that performed the best. Our best-performing ad featured a side-by-side comparison of EcoShine with a leading chemical cleaner, highlighting the natural ingredients, safety, and effectiveness of the product.

In addition to social media, we built a small but engaging landing page for EcoShine, complete with customer testimonials, before-and-after photos, and a clear, compelling call to action that encouraged visitors to purchase directly from the site. We offered a limited-time discount to incentivize first-time buyers, which helped us quickly capture leads and convert them into paying customers.

Within weeks, the engagement on social media began to soar. We saw hundreds of comments, shares, and likes from people genuinely interested in the product. Orders began pouring in, and in just three months, EcoShine saw a 300% increase in sales. The client was ecstatic, and more importantly, they realized that they could indeed compete with the big players by focusing on what made their product different and telling that story effectively.

I've got hundreds of similar stories where strategic marketing has turned struggling businesses around, whether it's a niche wellness product, a local cafe, or even my own vending machine business. The principles are always the same: find what makes you unique, communicate that clearly, and make sure the right people see it.

When I started my vending machine business, I took the same strategic approach. I knew I needed to make my machines stand out, not just blend in with the hundreds of other vending machines out there. I began with thoughtful branding, choosing colors and designs that would grab attention from afar. I added clear, attractive signage that spoke directly to customers' needs—like “Healthy Snacks for Busy Days” near office buildings or “Grab-and-Go Energy” at gyms.

Honestly, at first, I was hesitant to invest in marketing my machines. I wondered if marketing was really necessary for something as straightforward as vending machines. But I quickly discovered that even small businesses need smart promotion. Without it, even the best locations couldn’t deliver the results I wanted. I began to see my machines as mini-billboards, each one an opportunity to tell my brand’s story. I also applied my Internet marketing experience by leveraging social media to let people know where to find my machines and what unique products they offered.

Marketing doesn't just help in selling products; it builds a relationship with customers, earns their trust, and keeps them coming back. Even for something as simple as a vending machine, the right marketing strategy can turn a casual passerby into a regular customer.

Now, I'll share with you the strategies that have helped me grow my vending business, including branding, signage, and both traditional and online marketing techniques. These are practical steps you can take to make your machines stand out and attract more customers, whether in person or online.

Branding and Signage

Branding is all about creating a strong, memorable identity for your business—one that customers recognize and trust. Think about some of the most popular brands in the world, like Google, Coca-Cola, Apple, or Nike. Each of these brands has carefully crafted a unique identity that is instantly recognizable. Google, for instance, uses its playful and colorful logo to convey a sense of creativity and approachability. Those bright primary colors—blue, red, yellow, and green—are not just chosen at random; they help make Google feel friendly and accessible to users of all ages.

Coca-Cola, on the other hand, has built a powerful brand around its signature red color. The moment you see that particular shade of red, whether it's on a billboard, a bottle, or even a simple can, you probably think of Coca-Cola. Their branding is consistent across every touchpoint, from the classic cursive logo to the warm, joyful images they use in their advertisements. Red is a color often associated with energy, excitement, and passion, which aligns perfectly with Coca-Cola's brand message of sharing happiness and moments of enjoyment.

Apple's branding is all about simplicity, elegance, and innovation. Their sleek, minimalist design and use of clean, neutral colors like white, black, and silver give the brand a sophisticated, premium feel. Apple doesn't just sell devices; they sell a lifestyle—one that's modern, cutting-edge, and effortlessly cool. The simplicity of their branding reflects the simplicity they strive for in their user experience, making it easy for consumers to associate Apple with innovation and quality.

Nike's branding is built around the idea of empowerment and athletic excellence. Their black and white "swoosh" logo is simple, yet bold, representing speed, movement, and motivation. Nike's use of black is strong and dominant, creating a feeling of power and determination, while their bright accent colors, like neon green or bold orange, grab attention and stand out on the field or the street. Their tagline, "Just Do It," has become a mantra for athletes and fitness enthusiasts worldwide, instantly reminding people of Nike's promise to inspire and support personal achievement.

Ask yourself: How can you create this same kind of connection for your vending machines? What colors, logos, or messages can make them instantly recognizable and appealing to your customers? Think about how you want people to feel when they see your machines and how you can consistently communicate that through your branding.

Understand that branding goes beyond just a logo or a name; it involves everything from the design of your machines and signage to the way you communicate with your customers. A consistent color scheme, catchy tagline, or unique design can help people instantly associate your machines with quality and reliability. It's about creating a story and personality for your business, so customers feel a connection with what you offer.

Create a Unique Brand Identity

First, ask yourself: What makes my vending business different? Is it the types of snacks or drinks you offer, the locations of your machines, or the specific customers you cater to? Once you know what sets you apart, think about how you want people to feel when they see your machines. Do you want them to feel excited, relaxed, healthy, or maybe just happy to find a convenient snack?

Next, consider the visual elements of your brand. What colors represent the feeling you want to convey? For example, if you want to convey a sense of energy and fun, consider using bright, bold colors like reds, oranges, or yellows. If you're targeting a health-conscious audience, greens and whites might work better to represent freshness and simplicity. Remember, colors play a huge role in brand recognition—studies show that color can increase brand recognition by up to 80%[xxvii].

What about your logo? A logo should be simple but memorable. Think about how your logo will look on a vending machine, which is often viewed quickly and from a distance. A complex or overly detailed design might not be as effective as something bold and easy to understand at a glance. Your logo should represent your business's personality. Is it playful, professional, healthy, or something else? Choose fonts and symbols that match this personality.

Now, consider your brand's voice. This is how you communicate with your customers. Are you friendly and casual, or more formal and authoritative? Your tone should be consistent across all your communications, from the text on your vending machines to your social media posts. Consistency in your brand's voice helps to build trust and makes your business feel familiar to customers.

For my business, I wanted my brand to be all about convenience and fun. I chose bright blues and yellows for my machines because these colors are cheerful and eye-catching. Blue represents trust and reliability, while yellow is associated with happiness and energy. I designed a simple, modern logo with playful elements to make it approachable and memorable. My logo is a fun, dynamic shape with a smiling snack icon, which immediately conveys that my machines offer a quick, enjoyable snacking experience. I also use friendly, casual language in all my messaging to make customers feel welcome and at ease.

To create a unique brand identity for your vending business, start by defining what makes your business special and the emotions you want to evoke in your customers. Choose colors, fonts, and a logo that represent these qualities, and maintain a consistent tone of voice in all your communications. Your brand identity should make people feel something positive when they see your machines, helping them remember and choose your business over others.

Use Eye-Catching Signage

Signage is a key part of marketing your vending machines. It grabs people's attention, draws them closer, and can turn casual passersby into customers. But how do you create eye-catching signage that effectively promotes your vending machines?

First, consider your goal: What message do you want your sign to convey? Are you promoting a specific product, highlighting a special offer, or simply inviting people to take a look? Keep your message clear and concise. The fewer words, the better. A short, direct phrase like "Hungry? Grab a Snack!" or "Thirsty? Ice-Cold Drinks Here!" can quickly communicate what your vending machine offers. Make sure your main message is big and bold so it can be read easily from a distance.

Next, think about the design. What colors will make your sign stand out? Bright, contrasting colors tend to catch the eye more effectively. For example, red and yellow are attention-grabbing and can create a sense of urgency or excitement, while green and blue might suggest freshness and trustworthiness. You should also use large, easy-to-read fonts. Avoid overly decorative fonts that might be hard to decipher at a glance. Instead, choose clean, bold fonts that stand out and align with your brand's identity.

Where will you place your signage? Location is key. Place signs at eye level where they're easily seen by people walking by. If your machine is on a busy street, consider putting signs on nearby lampposts, walls, or bulletin boards. If it's in a building, use walls, columns, or doors that get a lot of foot traffic. The closer the sign is to the machine, the better—it can act as a direct invitation to check out what's inside.

For my vending machines, I created simple but eye-catching signs using bright blues and yellows to match my brand colors. I kept the text minimal—phrases like "Snack Attack? We've Got You Covered!" in big, bold letters. I also included images of the most popular snacks and drinks to give people a quick visual cue. My signs are positioned at eye level, and I always ensure they're in areas with high foot traffic.

One time, I noticed one of my machines was getting less traffic than others in a similar spot, I created a bright, colorful sign with simple text: "Hungry? Grab a Snack!" Sales jumped by nearly 30% in the first month!

To create your own eye-catching signage, start by defining a clear message and using bright colors that reflect your brand. Keep the text short, use large fonts, and strategically place your signs where people are most likely to see them.

Keep the Design Consistent

Consistency is key in branding, and it plays a crucial role in making your vending machines easily recognizable and memorable to customers. When your branding elements—such as colors, logos, and design—are consistent across all your machines, it creates a strong, cohesive identity that helps customers identify your brand, even if they encounter your machine for the first time.

To achieve branding consistency, start by establishing a clear visual identity for your vending machines. What are the key elements of your brand? This includes your color scheme, logo, fonts, and overall design style. Once you have these elements defined, use them uniformly across all your machines, signage, and social media. This ensures that every machine and content looks and feels like part of the same brand, reinforcing your business's identity.

Studies show that consistent branding can increase revenue by up to 23%[xxviii]. By maintaining a uniform look and feel across all my machines, I've noticed that my regular customers began actively seeking out my vending machines because they trusted the familiar brand. They recognized the consistent color scheme and logo, which gave them confidence in the quality and reliability of my machines.

Promoting Your Machines

Promoting your vending machines goes beyond simply placing them in high-traffic locations. It involves actively informing potential customers about where your machines are and why they should choose them over others. Effective promotion ensures that your vending machines attract attention, stand out from the competition, and drive sales.

To illustrate, consider the difference between just having a vending machine in a busy area versus actively promoting it. If you place a machine in a college campus, that's a great start, but if you want to maximize its success, you need to ensure that students know about it and are motivated to use it.

For example, you might place a vending machine in a student lounge but also run a targeted campaign using flyers and social media to let students know about the machine. You could create eye-catching posters with special promotions like "Get 10% off your first purchase!" and place them around campus, near the machine itself, and in common areas where students gather. This way, you're not just relying on the location; you're actively engaging with your target audience.

Similarly, let's say you have a vending machine in a busy office building or another high-traffic location. While the machine's location is convenient, promoting it involves more than that. You might send out a company-wide email introducing the new machine, offering a discount for employees, or placing a small stand with sample products in the break room. To get sample products, contact your product suppliers or distributors and request a small quantity of samples for promotional purposes.

Here's how you can approach sending out a company-wide email:

Identify the Right Contact: Start by reaching out to the office manager, facilities coordinator, or HR department. These individuals often handle internal communications and can help facilitate your promotional efforts. When contacting them, introduce yourself and your vending machine business, and explain how you'd like to work together to promote your machine.

Craft Your Email: Your email should be clear and concise, highlighting the benefits of your vending machine. Include details such as:

- **Introduction:** Briefly introduce your vending machine and its offerings.
- **Benefits:** Explain how it adds value to the employees or tenants, such as convenience, healthy snacks, or a variety of options.
- **Special Offer:** Mention any discounts or promotions available exclusively for the employees, like "Enjoy 10% off your first purchase!"
- **Call to Action:** Encourage recipients to visit the machine and try out the products.

Here's a sample email template:

Subject: New Vending Machine Now Available in Your Building!

Dear [Recipient's Name],

We are excited to announce that a new vending machine has been installed in the [specific location, e.g., break room or lobby] of your building! Our vending machine offers a variety of snacks and beverages designed to cater to your preferences.

To celebrate the launch, we're offering an exclusive 10% discount on your first purchase. Simply use the code WELCOME10 at checkout.

We hope you enjoy the convenience and variety our vending machine brings. If you have any questions or feedback, please feel free to reach out to us.

Best regards,

[Your Name]

[Your Contact Information]

[Your Company Name]

Negotiate This During Placement: When discussing placement with the establishment, mention that you would like to include a periodic (maybe, weekly or monthly) company-wide email or internal announcement as part of your agreement. Many companies have access to their employees' email addresses and can help spread the word. For example, gyms, schools, and office complexes often maintain contact lists that can be used to announce new amenities or services. However, some establishments might not agree to this request. In any case, you can still explore other promotional strategies such as placing eye-catching signs near the machine or offering special promotions directly to the customers.

These efforts make employees and customers aware of the machine's presence and encourage them to check it out.

Here are other ways I promote my vending machines:

Partnering with Local Businesses and Events

One of the best things I did was to partner with local businesses. For example, I reached out to a nearby gym and asked if I could place a vending machine inside. In return, I offered the gym a small percentage of the profits. This arrangement worked well for both of us—I gained a steady stream of health-conscious customers, and the gym earned extra revenue.

You can also promote your machines at local events. I once set up a temporary machine at a community fair, offering popular snacks and drinks. It was a great way to introduce my brand to a new audience and increase sales.

Offering Promotions and Discounts

Everyone loves a deal, and vending machine customers are no different. I started offering "Buy One, Get One Free" promotions on certain items, especially on slower sales days. I'd use simple stickers on the machine to announce these deals. Sales would often double on days when I ran these promotions.

Another method I used was offering a loyalty program. I used a software system that tracks purchases via credit or debit cards. Customers who bought from my machines five times could get their sixth snack for free. This helped build repeat customers and encouraged more sales.

Using QR Codes for Instant Access

Adding QR codes to your machines can help you engage with customers in new ways. I placed QR codes on the side of my machines that linked to a landing page where customers could see all the items available, get nutritional information, and even suggest new products they'd like to see. This simple addition made customers feel more connected and valued, and it boosted sales by around 15% in the first few months.

Leveraging Social Media and Online Marketing

Like I said before, online marketing isn't just for big brands; it can work wonders for vending machines, too. Social media and online platforms allow you to reach a broader audience and build a community around your brand.

Build a Presence on Social Media

I created accounts on Instagram, Facebook, and Twitter to showcase my vending machines. I posted pictures of new products, promotions, and the different locations of my machines. I also shared stories of customers enjoying their favorite snacks. Social media is a great way to interact with customers, get feedback, and build a loyal following.

Did you know that 71% of consumers are more likely to purchase from a brand they follow on social media[xxix]? I found this to be true as my follower count grew—I noticed more customers recognizing my brand and actively searching for my machines.

Run Targeted Ads Online

I also experimented with targeted ads on Facebook and Google. I set the ads to show up for people who were in the vicinity of my machines or who had searched for snacks or drinks nearby. It was a cost-effective way to attract local customers, and I saw an increase in sales when I ran these ads.

Utilize Google My Business

One thing I did early on was to list each of my vending machine locations on Google My Business. This allowed my machines to show up when people searched for snacks or drinks nearby. I'd encourage customers to leave positive reviews, which helped boost my rankings and attract more people to my machines.

Collaborate with Influencers or Local Celebrities

I always partner with local influencers who are popular in the areas where I have machines. One of them, a fitness blogger, mentioned my healthy snack options on her Instagram page, which led to a noticeable spike in sales at my machines located near gyms and sports centers. When I say influencers, I'm not talking about A-list celebrities. I'm referring to micro and nano influencers—people who have a strong presence in your local area and are well-regarded within their communities. These influencers often have smaller but highly engaged followings, making them more affordable and effective for local promotions. Collaborations like these can provide significant benefits, especially for local businesses looking to target specific audiences.

As you now know, marketing your vending business is not just about placing machines in the right spots—it's about making them stand out and attracting customers through smart branding, effective promotions, and strategic use of social media. With the right mix of in-person and online marketing tactics, you can create a recognizable brand, build a loyal customer base, and drive consistent sales growth. Remember, every small step counts—whether it's adding a sign, offering a discount, or posting a picture on Instagram.

Up next: After you've made the sales and are starting to see profits roll in, it's time to get smart about managing your money! In the next chapter, we'll explore how to set prices that balance profit with competitiveness, track every dollar coming in and going out, and handle tax considerations. Get ready for practical tips and strategies that will help you keep your vending business financially fit and thriving.

CHAPTER 9:
Financial Management

Pricing your products, whether in the vending machine business or any other industry, isn't just about slapping a number on something and hoping people will buy it. It's a strategic decision that can impact everything—from your ability to cover expenses to the long-term sustainability of your business. In many types of businesses, from retail to real estate, pricing has to reflect not only the value of what you're offering but also the costs involved in providing it. When you underprice, you may get more customers at first, but you might also end up struggling to cover your operating expenses.

In the early days of my vending business, I made the mistake of pricing some of my products too low in an effort to undercut a competitor nearby. I had a machine placed in a busy office building, and a competitor's machine, located just down the hall, had similar products. I was anxious to attract as many customers as possible, so without giving it much thought, I priced two popular items—bottled water and chips—lower than his. I sold water at $1, even though I was paying nearly 70 cents per bottle after factoring in shipping. I also set the price of chips at $1.25, which gave me a margin of about 30 cents. I figured the low prices would drive more traffic to my machine and leave my competitor in the dust.

At first, it seemed to work—sales of water and chips soared, and I noticed people started visiting my machine more often. But after a few weeks, I realized that while my machine was popular, I wasn't seeing the kind of profit I had expected. Sure, I was selling more, but by the time I covered the cost of the products, restocking, machine maintenance, and the rent I was paying for the prime location, my profit margin was razor-thin. I hadn't factored in the small markup I had left myself to reinvest in the business. I was essentially giving products away, with very little to show for it in return.

So, you see, pricing isn't just about attracting customers; it's about creating a balance between affordability and profitability. I had been so focused on getting more sales that I forgot the basic rule: pricing has to cover all your costs, with enough left over to make a decent profit. I adjusted my prices accordingly, raising the water to $1.50 and the chips to $1.75. While I lost a few sales initially, the change meant that the profits from each sale were enough to sustain the business and help it grow.

However, this experience taught me two valuable lessons. First, whether you're selling a product or offering a service, pricing is more than just beating the competition. It's about ensuring that your business stays healthy in the long run.

The second lesson was a marketing strategy. Instead of pricing everything low, I strategically price certain popular products lower than my competitors to draw more attention to my machine. For example, in areas with a lot of foot traffic or offices, I'll price items like bottled water or chips just a little below the competition. This creates a buzz around my machine and gets people talking about how they can save money by buying from it.

The benefit of this strategy is that it can make your vending machine stand out in a crowded market. Customers are always looking for a deal, and even saving a small amount on frequently purchased items can make a big difference. Once people start coming to your machine for the lower-priced products, they're more likely to buy other items from you as well, even if those items are priced similarly to or slightly higher than your competitor's.

However, there is a disadvantage to this approach. Pricing some products too low for too long can hurt your overall profit, especially if those items are big sellers and cost you a lot to restock. You also have to be careful not to rely too heavily on this strategy because it can be hard to sustain over time. If you're always offering deep discounts on certain products, customers might come to expect it, and it can become difficult to raise prices later on without losing sales.

If you're going to use this strategy, my advice is to be selective. Choose just one or two popular items to price lower than the competition, and only do it in locations where you're confident it will make a difference. Make sure that your other products are priced appropriately to make up for the lower margins on those discounted items. This way, you can still attract customers with a good deal while keeping your overall profit healthy.

Don't run this promotion for too long. I typically run mine for around two to four weeks. The goal is to create a buzz and draw in new customers, but if you keep prices too low for too long, it can eat into your profit margins. By setting a time limit, you can drive sales without setting an expectation that those discounts will always be there. It also helps you assess if the strategy is working, allowing you to adjust or try something new without long-term losses.

To set the right prices, you need to look at a few key things:

Cost of Goods Sold (COGS): Calculate how much each product costs you, including shipping and taxes. For example, if a can of soda costs you 50 cents, you need to price it above that to make a profit.

Markup: Decide how much profit you want to make on each item. A common markup for vending machines is around 100%—which means if you buy a product for $1, you sell it for $2. But this can vary depending on your location, the type of product, and what competitors are charging.

- **Location Variations:**

  In a high-traffic location like a busy office complex or a school, customers are often willing to pay a bit more for the convenience. For example, you might buy a snack for $1 and sell it for $2.50 because people are willing to pay more for quick access. On the other hand, if your machine is placed in a more competitive environment, like a gym with multiple vending machines, your markup might need to be lower to attract customers. In this case, you could price that same $1 snack at $1.75 to stay competitive.

- **Product Variations:**

  Certain products allow for different levels of markup. For example, healthier snacks, such as protein bars, often carry higher price tags, and customers are willing to pay more for them, especially in places like gyms or health clubs. A $1.50 protein bar could easily sell for $3 in a gym vending machine. But for more common items, like bottled water or chips, you might need to keep the markup closer to 100%, depending on what people expect to pay. In a standard office location, a bottle of water might cost $1 to buy and sell for $2. In contrast, in a high-end gym, you could charge $2.50 or even $3.

- **Competitor Pricing:**

  Paying attention to what your competitors charge is key. If you're located near another vending machine that sells soda for $1.50, you probably wouldn't want to price your soda at $2, or you risk losing customers. In such a case, you may decide to match or slightly undercut your competition by pricing your soda at $1.50 or $1.40. However, if you're the only machine in a location, like a small office with no nearby options, you have more flexibility. You could mark up that $1 soda to $2 without losing customers.

Ultimately, your markup strategy depends on where your machine is located, the type of customers you're serving, and how much competition you have. It's all about finding the right balance to maximize profits without pushing away customers due to high prices.

Tracking Income and Expenses

Keeping a close eye on your income and expenses is the backbone of running a successful vending business. In the early days, I used to track everything manually. I would check my machines weekly, count the coins and cash, and then enter everything into a spreadsheet. It worked fine when I had just two machines. But as my business grew and I invested in more advanced vending machines, I needed a more efficient way to stay organized.

That's when I started using vending management software, which completely transformed how I managed my operations. One tool I rely on is VendSoft, which offers a comprehensive solution for tracking every aspect of my vending business.

VendSoft syncs with my card-enabled machines and generates daily reports showing exactly how much each machine has earned, down to the penny. I no longer have to guess which machines are performing well or manually count cash—everything is tracked in real-time. The software also integrates seamlessly with my inventory, notifying me when stock is low. This is incredibly helpful for machines in high-traffic areas where items sell out quickly.

By having a clear view of income and expenses, I can immediately see where money is coming in and going out. For example, VendSoft breaks down sales by product and location, helping me understand which snacks and drinks are the most popular at each site. This data allows me to make informed decisions on what to restock and even adjust prices based on performance. It also helps me track expenses like rent for machine locations, cost of goods, and maintenance costs, giving me a full picture of my business's financial health.

With this level of control and insight, I'm able to optimize each machine, reduce waste, and ensure that every product I stock contributes to my bottom line. Plus, with the mobile app, I can check on all my machines from anywhere—whether I'm traveling or just away from my computer. This software has truly been a game changer in managing both my income and expenses, allowing me to grow my business efficiently.

Now, if you're starting small, tracking your finances in a simple Excel sheet or Google Sheets can work too. Just make sure you record:

- Income per machine (weekly or monthly, depending on how often you collect the cash)
- Expenses like purchasing new stock, transportation costs, and maintenance fees
- Net profit after all costs are deducted

Here is what my typical spreadsheet looks like:

Machine Location	Category	Product	Weekly Income ($)	Stock Cost ($)	Transportation Cost ($)	Maintenance Cost ($)	Total Expenses ($)	Net Profit ($)
Gym	Beverages	Coca-Cola Soda	$ 200.00	$ 50.00	$ 10.00	$ 5.00	$ 65.00	$ 135.00
Gym	Snacks	Lay's Chips	$ 180.00	$ 45.00	$ 10.00	$ 5.00	$ 60.00	$ 120.00
School	Beverages	Aquafina Water	$ 150.00	$ 30.00	$ 12.00	$ 5.00	$ 47.00	$ 103.00
School	Snacks	Snickers Candy	$ 160.00	$ 40.00	$ 12.00	$ 5.00	$ 57.00	$ 103.00
Office	Beverages	Tropicana Juice	$ 220.00	$ 60.00	$ 8.00	$ 5.00	$ 73.00	$ 147.00
Office	Snacks	Doritos Chips	$ 200.00	$ 50.00	$ 8.00	$ 5.00	$ 63.00	$ 137.00
Mall	Beverages	Pepsi Soda	$ 230.00	$ 55.00	$ 15.00	$ 5.00	$ 75.00	$ 155.00
Mall	Snacks	KitKat Chocolate	$ 190.00	$ 40.00	$ 15.00	$ 5.00	$ 60.00	$ 130.00

This spreadsheet breaks down the financial tracking of four vending machines placed in various locations: a gym, a school, an office, and a mall. It tracks several categories of products, including beverages and snacks, with specific brands like Coca-Cola, Pepsi, Aquafina, and popular snacks like Lay's Chips and Snickers Candy.

Columns:

- **Machine Location:** Shows where each vending machine is located.
- **Category:** Divides the products into broad categories (e.g., Beverages, Snacks).
- **Product:** Lists the specific brand products being sold (e.g., Coca-Cola, Lay's Chips).
- **Weekly Income ($):** This is the total income generated from the product for the week.

- **Stock Cost ($):** Represents the cost to purchase the stock (wholesale prices).
- **Transportation Cost ($):** The cost of restocking the vending machine, which includes fuel or delivery fees.
- **Maintenance Cost ($):** Fixed weekly cost for minor repairs or upkeep (this can vary but is kept constant for simplicity here).
- **Total Expenses ($):** Sum of stock, transportation, and maintenance costs.
- **Net Profit ($):** The remaining profit after subtracting total expenses from weekly income.

Summary:

For example, the Coca-Cola soda in the gym location generated a weekly income of $200. After deducting $50 for stock, $10 for transportation, and $5 for maintenance, the total expenses amounted to $65, leaving a net profit of $135. Similarly, each location and product have its own income and expenses, showing how much profit you make per item and location.

This type of spreadsheet can help you easily track your income and expenses, giving you a clear understanding of your vending machine business's financial health.

Tax Considerations and Record-Keeping

As with any business, managing taxes is an essential part of keeping things running smoothly. From day one, I understood the importance of keeping my finances in order because I already had experience managing taxes for my other ventures. Whether it's my real estate projects or internet marketing business, keeping personal and business expenses separate has always been a priority, and I knew it would be the same for my vending machines. This approach made tax season a lot easier, as I already had everything organized, from deductible expenses to clear records of income and costs.

Here are some key tax considerations for vending machine operators:

Sales Tax: Depending on your state, you may need to collect sales tax on each item you sell. It's essential to know the local laws, as some states tax snacks and beverages while others do not. I've found that keeping a separate column in my financial records for sales tax helps me track what I owe at the end of each quarter.

Deductible Expenses: You can deduct the cost of goods sold, machine maintenance, restocking trips, and even mileage if you're driving to check on your machines. Consult with a tax advisor to know exactly what's deductible in your area. This has helped me save a lot on taxes by maximizing my deductions.

Record-Keeping: Keep all your receipts and invoices organized. I've set up a digital folder where I scan every receipt as soon as I get it. That way, come tax season, everything is in one place.

The IRS requires that you keep good records for at least three years in case of an audit, so having a system in place is critical.

Managing the financial side of your vending business might seem complicated, but with the right tools and habits, it becomes second nature. Start by setting prices that reflect your costs and market demand, then stay on top of your income and expenses with consistent tracking. Finally, keeping your tax obligations in check will help you avoid headaches down the road and ensure that your business stays profitable.

Up next: Once you've got your vending business running smoothly and the profits start rolling in, the next step is thinking about growth. In the next chapter, you will learn how to scale your business—whether it's expanding to new locations, hiring employees to help manage operations, or tapping into new markets and opportunities. I'll share my own experience of when I knew it was the right time to expand and the strategies I used to make it happen. Get ready to take your vending business to the next level!

CHAPTER 10:
Scaling Your Business

Once your vending business is steady and bringing in consistent profits, the next logical step is to think about growth. Expanding your business can mean many things: adding more machines, exploring new locations, hiring employees, or even looking into new markets. But how do you know when the time is right, and how do you manage it effectively?

In any business, scaling is a sign of success. Think of some of the world's top brands—companies like Amazon, Starbucks, or Nike didn't start as global giants. Amazon started as an online bookstore, but once the company mastered that niche, it expanded into selling everything from electronics to groceries, and now it dominates multiple industries. Starbucks, initially a small coffee shop in Seattle, gradually grew into an international chain, opening new locations year after year. And Nike, which began as a modest shoe brand, expanded into clothing, accessories, and sports gear, making it one of the most recognizable names in the world. These brands didn't become successful by staying small. They grew strategically, expanded their reach, and captured new markets while staying true to their core values.

Scaling is about recognizing opportunities to grow and seizing them at the right moment. Whether it's introducing new products, opening more locations, or targeting a broader audience, expansion is how businesses evolve. It allows them to increase their revenue, build stronger customer bases, and stay competitive in the long run.

The vending machine business is no different. It might seem simple, but it's a business that thrives on expansion. Once you've got a few machines that are running smoothly and turning a profit, adding more machines in similar locations can help you multiply your success. The more visible your machines are in different places, the more familiar people become with your brand—and the more likely they are to seek out your machines for snacks, drinks, or other products. Scaling up a vending business means more revenue, a broader customer base, and more opportunities to partner with new locations.

I've seen the importance of scaling firsthand, not just in my vending machine business but in my digital marketing business as well. I started by working with small businesses in Atlanta, focusing on building their online presence and increasing their visibility. As my clients saw results and word of mouth spread, I expanded into other cities and eventually to other states. Now, my agency serves both small and big businesses across the world. It wasn't just about taking on more clients—it was about finding new opportunities, adapting to different markets, and continuously improving my services to meet growing demands.

The lessons I've learned in digital marketing—about timing, scaling, and managing growth—are the same principles I apply to my vending machine business. Knowing when to expand and how to manage that growth is key to long-term success, no matter the industry.

When and How to Expand

The first thing to consider when thinking about expanding is whether your current machines are consistently performing well. Are they bringing in steady revenue? Are your expenses covered with room for profit? If you're regularly having to restock because products are selling quickly, that's a good sign it's time to expand. But if you're still struggling to make consistent sales, it might be better to wait before adding more machines.

In my case, I decided to expand after noticing that some of my machines were constantly running out of stock, especially in high-traffic areas like gyms and office complexes. The demand was clearly there, so adding more machines made sense. I didn't rush into it, though. Before expanding, I evaluated the cost of new machines, the additional restocking requirements, and the time it would take to manage more locations.

When you're ready to grow, start by looking for locations similar to your top-performing spots. If gyms work well for you, explore other gyms in your area. If office complexes are your niche, find more offices to target. Sticking to what's already working is a smart move, especially in the early stages of expansion. At the same time, don't overlook new opportunities in different kinds of locations like schools, apartment complexes, or even retail stores. Each location has its unique set of customers, and learning how to tap into those different markets can be a great way to grow.

That said, scaling isn't compulsory! Not everyone feels the need to grow their business beyond a certain point, and that's perfectly fine. You may have started your vending business with a specific goal in mind, whether it's a certain number of machines or a specific income target. If you've reached that goal and feel content, there's no pressure to expand just because you can. Sometimes, staying small and manageable is the right choice, especially if it aligns with your lifestyle or personal values.

In fact, there are valid reasons why you might choose not to expand, even if your machines are doing well and there's high demand. Scaling up often requires more time, more capital, and more management responsibilities. You might not want to take on the additional workload, or maybe the idea of managing a larger operation doesn't fit with your long-term vision. It's also possible that you're balancing other personal or professional goals and don't want to spread yourself too thin by growing your vending business.

This is a lesson I've applied in my real estate business as well. I set a goal for myself to flip no more than five houses in a year, even though I had the opportunity to do more. The reason was simple: I wanted to maintain a balance between running my business and having time for my personal life. Expanding beyond that would have meant working longer hours and taking on more stress than I was willing to handle at the time. For me, it wasn't just about profits—it was about living the kind of life I wanted, where I had time for both business and personal interests.

It's understandable why some people might decide not to scale their business for personal reasons. You might have a full-time job, other business ventures, or family commitments that take up your time. Growth is great, but it's not always the right choice for everyone, and there's nothing wrong with keeping your business at a size that you can comfortably manage. It all comes down to your priorities and what makes the most sense for your life and business goals.

Hiring and Managing Employees

As your business grows, you may find it difficult to handle everything on your own. When you start adding more machines or managing multiple locations, hiring employees can help lighten the load. But knowing when to hire is just as important as knowing when to expand.

I hired my first employee when I had about 10 machines and realized I was spending too much time restocking them and not enough time on other areas of the business. Managing all the logistics became overwhelming, from keeping track of inventory to driving back and forth between locations. I started with one part-time employee to help with restocking and basic maintenance. This allowed me to shift my focus to finding new locations, negotiating contracts, and tracking the overall performance of the business.

This first hire turned out to be a game-changer. She was reliable, efficient, and had great attention to detail. On top of that, she already had another part-time job, so she was familiar with managing her time well. Plus, she lived close to all the machines I assigned her to manage, which made the job much more convenient. Her proximity and dedication helped streamline operations and set a standard for all future hires.

From the start, she was proactive in identifying problems before they became serious, like noticing a machine needed more frequent cleaning or seeing that a certain product wasn't selling as well. She became the model template for how I now hire employees. Over time, I've hired more than 50 employees across various locations, and every time I bring someone new on board, I look for the same traits I saw in my first hire: a strong work ethic, dependability, and a sense of ownership over the job.

The Wrong Hire Can Hurt Growth

Hiring the wrong person can hold back your business's growth in more ways than one. For instance, I once hired someone who seemed like a good fit during the interview, but red flags started popping up right away. They were often late, disorganized, and didn't follow the procedures I had in place. These issues caused delays in restocking, customer complaints, and even lost sales.

From that experience, I've learned to watch for red flags during the hiring process, like a lack of punctuality or failure to follow instructions. If someone can't show up on time for the interview or misses basic directions, it's likely they'll do the same on the job. These behaviors are often signs of larger issues like poor time management or a lack of commitment, which can be disastrous for a vending business that relies on efficiency and attention to detail.

Step-by-Step Guide to Hiring

To avoid these pitfalls, I've developed a step-by-step process for hiring employees, specifically tailored to the vending machine business:

Step 1: Identify Your Needs

Before hiring, figure out exactly what you need help with. Is it restocking machines, handling maintenance, or customer service? Understanding the specific tasks will help you find the right person for the job. A common mistake is hiring someone without a clear job description, which can lead to confusion and unmet expectations.

Step 2: Write a Detailed Job Description

Outline the duties and expectations clearly. Include the number of hours, pay, and any other details like location proximity. Be upfront about the physical demands of the job, like lifting heavy boxes or traveling between locations. This helps filter out candidates who aren't a good fit.

Step 3: Screen for Red Flags

During the interview, pay close attention to red flags like tardiness or vague answers about past employment. Ask specific questions about their experience with tasks similar to those in the vending business. For example, have they ever managed inventory or done maintenance work? Vague or overconfident responses can signal a lack of experience.

Step 4: Start with a Trial Period

It's a good idea to start new hires with a trial period of a few weeks to a few months. This gives you time to evaluate their performance without committing long-term. If they don't meet expectations during this period, it's easier to part ways before issues start affecting your business.

Step 5: Provide Clear Instructions and Feedback

Once hired, make sure to train them thoroughly. Show them exactly how you want tasks done, from restocking procedures to handling maintenance issues. Offer feedback regularly, especially during the trial period. Lack of feedback is a common mistake that can leave employees confused about whether they're meeting expectations.

What to Do When Performance Falls Short

Not every hire will be a perfect fit. If an employee isn't meeting expectations, address the issue sooner rather than later. Have a direct conversation about what needs improvement, whether it's punctuality, attention to detail, or something else. If the problem persists, it may be time to let them go and find someone better suited for the role. Keeping an underperforming employee can hurt your business in the long run by causing inefficiencies and even damaging relationships with customers.

Payment and Contracts

When it comes to payment, I started by offering $15 per hour for part-time work, which increased with experience and responsibilities. My top performers now make anywhere from $20 to $25 per hour, and I provide incentives like bonuses for good performance. For example, if a machine consistently sells out, they receives a bonus of $50 for keeping it fully stocked and clean. This system has motivated my employees to stay on top of their tasks and take pride in the machines they manage.

However, wages can vary depending on the type of contract. For part-time workers, you might be paid hourly, while full-time employees may be on salary. Be sure to consider the local regulations around wages and contracts in your area. For example, some regions have specific requirements for benefits or overtime pay based on the type of contract you offer.

How to Determine How Much to Pay

When hiring, it's essential to figure out how much you can afford to pay your employees while ensuring your business remains profitable. Let’s start with some simple math. Suppose a vending machine brings in $1,000 a month in sales. If your profit margin after expenses (like inventory, maintenance, and rent) is 40%, that leaves you with $400 in profit. If you hire an employee to manage five machines, that’s $2,000 in total profit. If they work part-time for 20 hours a week at $15 per hour, you’ll pay them around $1,200 per month (including payroll taxes and other expenses). After paying their salary, you’re left with $800 in profit, and you’ve freed up your own time to focus on growing the business further.

However, how much you pay also depends on the type of contract you offer. For example, if you hire an employee as a full-time worker, you may need to offer benefits like health insurance, paid time off, and comply with other local labor regulations. These additional costs need to be factored into the overall compensation package. On the other hand, if you hire part-time workers or independent contractors, you may avoid some of these obligations, but you'll need to stay aware of local laws to ensure you're in compliance with labor regulations. Independent contractors, for example, often have more flexibility in setting their hours, but they may charge higher rates because they're responsible for their own benefits and taxes.

Another important consideration when determining pay is the demand in the job market. If you're offering competitive wages, you're likely to attract a larger pool of qualified candidates. Research shows that companies offering better compensation tend to draw more talent, leading to better employee performance and retention[xxx]. Although this research often focuses on large corporations, it applies to small businesses as well, including those in the vending industry. Paying higher-than-average wages can set your business apart and reduce the costs of turnover, which can often be higher than the extra pay you'd offer to keep good employees.

You should also keep an eye on the local job market. In areas where there's a shortage of labor or a high demand for part-time workers, you may need to offer higher wages to stay competitive. On the other hand, if you're in an area where job demand is low, you might have more flexibility in setting wages, but be careful not to underpay and risk losing potential talent to other businesses.

Ultimately, the goal is to strike a balance between fair compensation for your employees and maintaining a healthy profit for your business. By considering contract types, compliance with local regulations, and market demand, you'll be able to set wages that benefit both your employees and your business.

Delegating Tasks

When hiring, think about what tasks you want to delegate first. Is it restocking machines, handling customer service, or doing maintenance? Hiring someone to take over these tasks can give you more time to grow the business. In my case, I started with restocking because that was the most time-consuming part. I provided my new hire with a detailed checklist to follow at each location, which included tasks like:

- Checking for expired products
- Cleaning the machine, especially the glass and buttons
- Monitoring stock levels and recording which items sell the most
- Restocking based on current inventory and sales trends

Clear expectations from the beginning ensure there's no confusion about their responsibilities.

Managing Employees

Managing employees requires regular communication and setting clear expectations. In my case, I set up a system where employees reported to me weekly on their progress. Every week, they would fill out a report detailing which machines they serviced, how many products were restocked, any issues they encountered (like a broken coin mechanism or slow sales for a particular item), and any ideas they had for improving the process. These reports allowed me to keep track of what was happening without having to visit each location myself.

To encourage accountability and performance, I also implemented a bonus system. Employees earned bonuses based on how well the machines they managed were performing. For example, if a machine's sales exceeded a certain target—let's say $500 per week—they'd receive a $50 bonus for keeping the machine fully stocked and clean. This system motivated my team to ensure the machines were always in top shape, and it boosted overall sales across the board.

I remember one employee in particular who managed a machine at a gym. She consistently kept the machines stocked with popular products and made sure they were spotless. Her machines quickly became the top earners, and her performance bonuses easily added up to $200 per month. This success pushed her to keep exceeding expectations.

However, not every employee delivers this level of performance. When an employee doesn't meet expectations, it's crucial to address the issue right away. Start by having a direct conversation. Ask them if they are facing any challenges, whether it's time management, unclear instructions, or other difficulties. Sometimes, an employee may simply need more training or clearer guidance.

If performance issues persist despite feedback and support, you'll need to take further action. This can include implementing a probation period where specific improvements must be made within a set time frame. Be clear about the consequences if performance doesn't improve, such as reducing hours or even letting them go if necessary.

The key is to balance fairness and accountability. While you should provide opportunities for growth and improvement, it's important not to let underperformance negatively affect your business. Keeping underperforming employees around for too long can lead to missed sales, poor machine upkeep, and lower team morale.

If you're unsure how to implement a reporting system or bonus structure, start simple. Even a basic weekly check-in where your employee gives a verbal or written update can go a long way. The key is staying in the loop without micromanaging. As you scale, consider using software to track employee performance and automate reporting.

Scaling through hiring is about finding the right people, paying them fairly, keeping them motivated, and addressing underperformance when necessary. With the right team in place, you'll free up more of your time to continue growing your vending business.

Exploring New Markets and Opportunities

As your vending business grows, it's also a good idea to think about branching into new markets. If you've been successful with snack machines, for example, you could consider expanding into other types of machines like coffee or healthy meal vending. Or, if you've focused mainly on office complexes, you might want to explore other locations like airports, hospitals, or schools.

I've mentioned this several times, but it's been one of the most profitable decisions I've made since starting my business: expanding into healthier snack options. In certain gym locations, I noticed that customers were more drawn to health-conscious products. So, I introduced a few healthy snack machines alongside my regular ones. The response was overwhelmingly positive, and this diversification allowed me to reach a new customer base without having to overhaul my entire business model.

Another way to explore new opportunities is by keeping an eye on trends. For example, the demand for contactless payments has surged in recent years. Offering machines that accept mobile payments or cards can set you apart from competitors who only accept cash. In fact, after upgrading my machines to accept mobile payments, I saw an increase in sales because customers found it more convenient.

You could also consider branching into corporate partnerships. For example, some companies may want vending machines that align with their employee wellness programs, offering healthy snacks or even fitness-related products. By positioning your vending business as a solution for their needs, you can open up a whole new revenue stream.

Scaling your vending business is an exciting step, but it requires careful planning. First, ensure your current machines are performing well before expanding into new locations. If you find yourself stretched thin, hiring an employee to take over restocking or maintenance can help free up your time to focus on growth. Finally, don't be afraid to explore new markets and adapt to emerging trends, whether that means offering healthier options or embracing the latest technology.

Up next: We'll cover how to analyze sales data, optimize your product mix, and implement seasonal and promotional strategies that work. Whether you're looking to fine-tune your offerings or make the most of special promotions, the next chapter will show you how small changes can lead to big results. Maximizing profits isn't just about selling more—it's about selling smarter, and this is where you'll learn how.

CHAPTER 11:
Maximizing Profits

Once your vending machines are up and running, the next natural question is: how do you maximize profits? This is something all business owners face, whether you're selling products in a store, running a service-based business, or, in this case, managing vending machines. It's not just about making more sales, but about getting the most value out of every transaction. You want each machine to be as efficient and profitable as possible, and that requires more than just putting products in and collecting money. It's about strategy, insight, and continuous improvement.

I learned this early on when I started my first digital marketing company. Back then, I thought it was all about onboarding as many clients as possible. I was taking on every project I could, working with businesses of all sizes across Atlanta. But over time, I realized that more clients didn't always mean more profit. I had to start analyzing the value of each client, looking at which ones brought in the most revenue versus how much time and resources they consumed. That shift in focus changed how I approached my business entirely. Instead of chasing numbers, I started to optimize how I worked with each client, making smarter decisions about which projects to take on and how to serve them best.

This same mindset applies to the vending machine business. It's not just about placing more machines or stocking more products. It's about looking at the data, understanding what sells, and fine-tuning your approach. Maybe some of your machines are doing great, while others aren't pulling in as much revenue. Or perhaps you're stocking items that don't move as quickly as you thought they would, tying up valuable space. These are all things you can tweak to boost your profits without necessarily adding new machines or locations.

For example, when I placed my first few vending machines, I thought it was a simple matter of stocking popular items and collecting the cash. It wasn't long before I realized that certain products were selling much faster than others, while some machines were performing better simply because of where they were located. By analyzing this data, I was able to adjust my product mix, ensuring that I wasn't wasting space on items that weren't selling. I also learned to time my restocks better, which helped keep the machines full and customers satisfied.

Keep reading as you will learn the specifics of how you can analyze your sales data, optimize your product mix, and use seasonal or promotional strategies to keep your vending machines profitable. Just like with any business, small adjustments can lead to big results. By understanding these key areas, you'll be able to make smarter decisions that will not only increase sales but also ensure that you're getting the most out of every machine you operate.

Analyzing Sales Data

The first step to maximizing your profits is understanding what's working and what's not. This means taking a close look at your sales data to spot patterns, trends, and opportunities for improvement. Are certain products flying off the shelves while others barely move? This kind of insight is key to making smart decisions about your inventory, pricing, and product selection.

When I first started, just like what most newbies do, I assumed I knew what people wanted—snacks, drinks, and candy. But I quickly realized that different locations had different preferences. For example, in office complexes, soda sales were consistently higher than snack sales. I didn't pay much attention to this at first, but after noticing this trend over a few months, I made a change. I decided to reduce the snack options that weren't moving and added more drinks, especially popular choices like flavored waters and energy drinks. This one small adjustment led to a 20% increase in sales for those machines.

If you don't analyze your data, you might miss opportunities like this. You could be stocking products that aren't selling or missing out on items your customers actually want. That's why it's essential to regularly review your sales data to identify which items are performing well and which are taking up space without bringing in revenue.

How to Analyze Sales Data with Software

If you're using vending management software, this process becomes a lot easier. These programs do most of the heavy lifting for you. They track everything from which products are selling the most to when your machines need restocking and how much each machine is making. This gives you a clear, real-time view of your business performance, without having to manually check every machine.

Like I have mentioned many times throughout this book, the software I use, VendSoft, syncs with my machines and provides me with daily reports. I can see which items are selling out fast, which products I need to restock, and which machines are lagging behind in sales. The software also alerts me when stock is running low or if there's been an issue with one of the machines. Having all this data in one place saves me a lot of time, and it helps me make better decisions on which products to focus on.

But what if you've hired someone to manage your machines? If someone else is in charge of restocking, it's crucial that they keep detailed records. This includes noting which products are low, how much cash or card payments were collected, and any issues with the machine. For older machines that cannot be integrated with software, I always make sure my employees use a checklist that tracks sales, product stock, and any maintenance needed for the machines. This way, I still have the data I need, even if I'm not personally checking each machine.

If you're not using software yet, you can start by keeping a simple spreadsheet. Record your weekly or monthly sales, track how often you restock each machine, and note which products are selling fast or slow. Over time, you'll be able to spot trends—like maybe bottled water sells more during summer, or candy sales spike around the holidays.

How to Analyze Sales Data Without Software

Let's say you don't have vending management software yet. You can still gather and analyze your data manually using spreadsheets. Here's a step-by-step process to help you get started:

Set Up a Spreadsheet: Create a table in Excel or Google Sheets with columns for the date, product name, quantity sold, machine location, and total sales per product. If you're restocking once a week, fill out the spreadsheet weekly.

Track Your Best Sellers: After a few weeks or months, sort the data by quantity sold. This will help you identify your top-selling products. If you see that chips or a certain brand of soda consistently ranks higher than others, you'll know to keep those items in stock.

Eliminate Low Sellers: On the flip side, if you notice certain products are barely selling, consider replacing them with something else. Maybe energy drinks aren't popular in an office building, but they might sell better in a gym. Tracking this over time allows you to fine-tune your inventory.

Watch for Trends: Seasonal trends can also emerge from your data. Maybe sales of hot drinks like coffee spike in the winter months, or ice-cold sodas sell out fast in the summer. Adjust your product mix based on these trends.

Calculate Restocking Frequency: Another thing to track is how often you're restocking each machine. Machines in high-traffic areas may need to be restocked more often than those in quieter locations. If you're restocking too frequently, it might be time to add another machine at that location to meet demand.

What to Expect from Your Employees

If you've hired someone to manage your machines, make sure they follow a structured system. Provide them with a restocking checklist that covers everything from counting cash and tracking product levels to noting any issues with the machine. You'll want them to report back to you regularly—whether it's through the vending software or manually—so you can review the data.

For example, when my first employee took over restocking for a few machines, I had her fill out a simple form after each visit. She noted the products she restocked, how much money was collected, and any issues she saw (like jams or faulty card readers). At the end of each week, she emailed me her report, which I then plugged into my spreadsheet. This helped me stay informed and make data-driven decisions, even though I wasn't physically checking every machine.

Here's a simple and clear restocking checklist that you can provide to your employees to ensure everything is handled properly during their visits to manage the vending machines. You can choose to do this digitally or print hard copies on paper. Keep in mind that the former will cost more.

Vending Machine Restocking Checklist

Employee Name: ___________________

Date: ___________________

Machine Location: ___________________

1. Cash Collection:

☐ Count the cash in the machine and note the total amount collected.

☐ Record any card sales or payments made via electronic methods (if applicable).

2. Product Stocking:

☐ Check current stock levels of all products.

☐ Restock products that are running low.

☐ Ensure products are placed with the soonest expiration dates at the front.

☐ Verify that all product prices are correct and visible.

3. Expiration Dates:

☐ Check the expiration dates of all items.

☐ Remove and discard any expired products.

☐ Record the number of expired items discarded for each product.

4. Machine Condition:

☐ Inspect the machine for any visible issues (e.g., jammed products, card reader problems, bill acceptor issues).

☐ Test the machine by purchasing a product to ensure it's working properly.

☐ Clean the machine exterior (wipe down screen, buttons, and product window).

5. Customer Complaints or Feedback:

☐ Check for any customer complaints or notes left near the machine.

☐ Record any customer feedback or issues reported.

6. Report Back:

☐ Submit a sales report, including:

Total cash collected.

Card payments (if applicable).

Number of items restocked.

Number of expired items removed.

Any maintenance issues identified.

☐ Report any machine issues that need fixing immediately.

7. Other Notes:

☐ Record any additional information (special requests, unusual sales patterns, or any other observations).

Signature: ___________________

Next Scheduled Visit: ___________________

How to Go Digital with Your Checklist

Google Forms or Microsoft Forms:

- You can easily convert this checklist into a digital form using free tools like Google Forms or Microsoft Forms. Both platforms allow you to create checkboxes for each task, and the completed checklist can be submitted and saved online.
- Employees can fill out the form on their smartphones or tablets while they're restocking machines.
- All responses are automatically saved in a spreadsheet, making it easier for you to track the data, analyze trends, and generate reports.

Vending Management Software:

- Many vending management systems, like VendSoft or ParLevel, have built-in digital checklists and tracking features. These programs allow employees to record tasks such as cash collection, restocking, and maintenance issues directly in the app.
- The data syncs in real-time, so you can monitor what's happening with your machines remotely, track progress, and get notifications when there's an issue that needs attention.

Project Management Tools:

- Tools like Trello, Asana, or Monday.com can be used to create checklists for each machine location. You can assign tasks to specific employees, set deadlines for visits, and track their progress.
- Employees can upload photos or notes directly into the app, allowing for a more detailed record of what's happening at each machine.

By using vending management software, or even a well-organized manual system, you'll be able to make informed decisions that improve your overall business performance. You'll know exactly which products are your top performers, which machines need attention, and where your opportunities for growth are. All of this can help you maximize profits without the guesswork.

Optimizing Your Product Mix

Not every location has the same demand, so it's essential to tailor your product mix to fit the preferences of your customers. In vending, a one-size-fits-all approach rarely works. A machine in a gym is going to have very different product requirements than one in an office or a school. For example, in a gym, customers are typically health-conscious, so healthier options like protein bars, flavored water, or even low-sugar energy drinks tend to perform better than chips or soda. Meanwhile, in schools, you'll find that juice boxes, granola bars, and snack packs are more popular because they cater to students looking for something quick and tasty between classes.

At one point, I decided to expand by adding two new machines to my fleet. I placed one in a newly opened gym and the other in a bustling office building. The differences in customer preferences were immediately noticeable. The gym crowd went straight for protein shakes, electrolyte drinks, and healthier snacks like veggie chips, while the office workers had different needs. They preferred items like iced coffee, granola bars, and trail mix. By adjusting the product mix to cater specifically to these preferences, I was able to boost sales in both locations.

Testing and Adjusting

Another key to optimizing your product mix is to constantly test and adjust your offerings. What works well in one location may not work in another, and even within the same location, customer preferences can shift over time. Every few months, I introduce new products to gauge customer interest. Sometimes, it's seasonal—like adding hot cocoa in the winter or cold-pressed juices in the summer—or it could be a new brand of chips or a different flavor of protein bars.

For example, I once added a new line of organic, gluten-free cookies to a few machines in health-conscious areas, just to test how well they would perform. It turned out to be a hit in some locations but barely moved in others. The trial period helped me figure out where to keep the product and where to swap it for something else. This constant testing not only keeps the product mix relevant but also adds a sense of novelty for repeat customers who appreciate seeing new items.

Understanding the Customer

Listening to what customers actually want is critical. In some of my office locations, I've had employees of that organization leave notes asking for specific items like sparkling water or a certain brand of chips. Paying attention to these requests helped me fine-tune my offerings to better suit their tastes, and that boosted sales. Sometimes, a minor tweak—like switching out regular bottled water for sparkling water—can make a big difference in overall profits.

Optimizing your product mix isn't just about putting random items in the machine and hoping they sell. It's about carefully analyzing your customers' preferences, testing new products, and making adjustments based on real-world feedback. By doing this, you not only increase sales but also build a loyal customer base who knows they can always find something they like in your vending machines. Keep things fresh, be willing to adapt, and you'll maximize your profits while keeping your customers happy.

Seasonal and Promotional Strategies

Seasons and holidays can have a big impact on what people buy. For example, in the summer months, cold drinks like water and sports drinks are top sellers, while in the winter, hot beverages like coffee or tea can see a spike in demand. You can also use holidays to your advantage. Around Halloween, for instance, adding themed candy or snacks can make your machine stand out.

I've used promotions during the slower winter months. One year, I ran a "Buy Two, Get One Free" promotion on snacks across several machines in schools and gyms. This simple promotion helped increase sales during a time when business was usually slower. Even though I was giving away a product, the volume of sales increased enough to cover the cost.

Another effective strategy I've used is teaming up with other local businesses. For example, during the back-to-school season, I partnered with a local school supply store to offer a discount code inside my machines. The code gave customers a small discount on their school supplies, and in return, the store promoted my machines in their marketing. This helped both businesses and attracted more customers.

As you can see, maximizing profits isn't just about selling more; it's about making sure every machine is operating at its best. Analyze your sales data regularly, adjust your product mix based on customer preferences, and don't be afraid to experiment with seasonal and promotional strategies. These small adjustments have made a big difference for me, and they can do the same for you.

Up next: You'll learn more about how cashless payment systems, remote monitoring, and new tech innovations can make managing your vending machines easier and more profitable. Discover how staying current with technology can give your business an edge and boost your bottom line.

CHAPTER 12:
Technology and Innovation

Throughout the chapters of this book, I've touched on various tech tools and innovations, both in the industry as a whole and specifically those that have helped my vending business run more smoothly and profitably. From vending management software to smart vending machines with digital displays, technology has played a big role in my business. But I decided to dedicate an entire chapter to technology and innovation because, in today's world, this area is constantly evolving. If you want to stay competitive and keep growing, you need to adapt. Technology can completely transform how you operate, and falling behind can have serious consequences.

Think about businesses like Blockbuster. At one time, it was the king of video rentals, with thousands of stores around the world. But they didn't keep up with the shift to digital streaming, and they paid the price. Meanwhile, Netflix, which started as a DVD rental service, embraced new technology and revolutionized how we watch TV and movies. Blockbuster had the chance to buy Netflix in its early days for 50 million dollars but passed, not realizing that technology was going to change the entire industry[xxxi]. As a result, Netflix thrived, and Blockbuster is now a thing of the past.

The lesson is clear: staying ahead of the curve and being willing to innovate is crucial for any business. In today's fast-paced world, those who fail to adapt risk becoming obsolete, while those who embrace new opportunities often thrive.

Now, I'm not saying I've never made mistakes, but one thing is for sure—I've always been tech-savvy. My friends even joke that I'm the first person to try out any new gadget or software before it's even hit the shelves. If there's a new tool or app that promises to make life easier, you can bet I'm all over it. I've always been the one in my friend group who gets excited about the latest innovations while others are still figuring out how to use the latest version. "Here comes the tech guinea pig," they laugh. But it's true. I'm always looking for ways to streamline things, and that curiosity has definitely helped my vending business.

When it comes to vending, keeping up with technology is not just a luxury—it's a necessity. From cashless payment systems to remote monitoring, the vending industry has seen major innovations over the years, and they've made it easier than ever to manage machines and increase profits. Imagine running your machines without knowing exactly what's selling, when restocking is needed, or whether a machine is broken until you physically visit the site. It's stressful and inefficient. But by integrating new tech, you can track all of this from your phone or computer and make informed decisions in real-time.

For me, embracing technology in my vending business wasn't just a smart move—it was the only move. I've always been the kind of person who sees the potential in new tools, and when I saw what technology could do for my machines, I jumped at the chance to implement it. From introducing cashless payments to using remote monitoring software, these innovations have not only helped me keep things running smoothly but have also boosted my sales and saved me countless hours of manual work.

Cashless Payment Systems

As the world moves toward digital transactions, offering cashless payment options is no longer just a nice-to-have—it's almost a necessity. Many people prefer the convenience of paying with a card, smartphone, or even a smartwatch rather than carrying cash. If your machines only accept cash, you might be missing out on a huge chunk of potential customers.

Recent studies support this shift in consumer behavior. Federal Reserve Payments Study found that in 2021, card payments made up approximately 77% of all noncash payments in the U.S., reflecting a steady shift away from cash transactions. This marked a significant increase from previous years, with card payment values growing at a rate of 10% per year between 2018 and 2021[xxxii]. Similarly, Square reported that 74% of U.S. sellers were accepting contactless payments by early 2021, compared to 64% the previous year. This shift highlights how crucial it is for your business to adopt cashless solutions to meet consumer expectations[xxxiii].

I remember when I first switched some of my machines to accept card payments. The difference was immediate—sales went up by about 30% in just a few weeks. It turns out that people are more likely to make impulse buys when they can pay with a card or tap their phone. Adding cashless payment options opened up a whole new customer base, especially in busy locations like office buildings and gyms.

Integrating cashless payment systems might seem intimidating, but it's easier than you might think. Most modern vending machines come with the option to install a card reader or a mobile payment device. If you have older machines, there are retrofit kits available that can add these features without replacing the entire machine.

To access and install a retrofit kit for cashless payment systems, you can typically purchase these kits from vending machine manufacturers or third-party suppliers that specialize in vending technology. Many suppliers offer kits compatible with a wide range of older vending machines.

Once you have the kit, installation is usually straightforward. Most kits include detailed instructions and are designed to be plug-and-play, meaning you don't need extensive technical knowledge. The kit will come with a card reader or mobile payment device, a connection module, and any necessary cables. Simply follow the provided instructions to attach the card reader to the machine and connect it to the machine's payment system. In some cases, you may need to update the machine's software to ensure compatibility with the new system.

After installation, you'll need to configure the payment device by setting up an account with a payment processor, which will handle the transactions. This may involve linking the device to a cloud-based system where you can track sales and payments.

Of course, there are fees associated with processing card payments, usually around 1.5% to 3% per transaction. It's something to keep in mind when setting your prices, but the increase in sales usually outweighs the cost.

Remote Monitoring and Management

As your vending business grows, keeping track of all your machines can become a challenge. That's where remote monitoring comes in. With remote monitoring software, you can check on your machines from anywhere—whether you're at home, on vacation, or managing another part of your business.

I've mentioned before how vending management software has been a game-changer for me, allowing me to track sales, monitor stock levels, and keep an eye on my machines without physically being there. In fact, it's one of the reasons I was able to expand my business. With a real-time view of what's happening with each machine, I could make better decisions about restocking and adjusting product mixes.

One of the best things about remote monitoring is that it saves time and reduces wasted trips. Instead of driving out to check on a machine only to find it's fully stocked, the software tells you exactly when a machine needs attention. This not only helps with efficiency but also reduces fuel costs and wear on your vehicle.

If you've hired someone to handle restocking and maintenance, remote monitoring is a way to keep tabs on their work too. You can see if a machine was restocked properly, if there are any issues, and how much cash has been collected, all without being there in person.

When choosing remote monitoring software for your vending machines, there are several key factors to consider:

- **Compatibility:** Ensure the software is compatible with your vending machines, especially if you have a mix of older and newer models. Some platforms only work with specific types of machines, so verify that it supports all your equipment.
- **Features:** Different software solutions offer various features like real-time sales tracking, inventory monitoring, and alert systems for maintenance. Choose one that aligns with your specific business needs. If you want detailed analytics on which products are selling best or automated notifications when stock runs low, look for software with those capabilities.
- **User-Friendliness:** The software should have an intuitive interface that's easy to navigate. If you or your employees find the system too complicated, it might hinder productivity rather than improve it.
- **Cost:** Software can vary in price depending on its features. Some platforms charge a flat fee, while others may have a monthly subscription or per-machine cost. Be sure to factor this into your overall budget to ensure that it's cost-effective.
- **Integration with Payment Systems:** Many vending management software solutions also integrate with cashless payment systems, allowing you to track transactions more easily. Ensure that the software you choose supports the payment processors you use or plan to use.

- **Customer Support and Training:** It's essential to have access to strong customer support in case you encounter technical issues. Look for providers that offer comprehensive training resources and responsive customer service.

By considering these factors, you'll be able to select remote monitoring software that optimally supports your vending machine business's growth and efficiency.

Integrating New Technologies

Technology in the vending industry is always evolving, and staying ahead of the curve can give you a real advantage. In addition to cashless payments and remote monitoring, there are other innovations worth exploring.

For example, some machines come with touchscreen displays, allowing customers to browse products or even watch short ads while they wait. These digital displays can be used to showcase new products, promote special offers, or even earn extra income by selling ad space to local businesses.

Another growing trend is smart inventory systems that automatically track stock levels and send alerts when an item is running low. This can save time on inventory management and ensure that your machines are always stocked with the products your customers want.

The adoption of smart inventory systems is transforming the vending industry by streamlining inventory management and reducing operational costs. These systems, equipped with technologies like RFID and IoT sensors, automatically track stock levels and send real-time alerts when items are running low. This not only helps reduce manual labor but also ensures that your machines are consistently stocked with the products your customers demand.

The demand for automated inventory solutions is on the rise. A report by Global Market Insights predicts that the global inventory management software market will grow to over $6 billion by 2032, driven by the need for real-time tracking and reduced human error[xxxiv]. The increasing integration of smart technology in the vending sector reflects a broader trend toward digital transformation in supply chains, providing operators with better accuracy and control over their stock.

Incorporating these systems can significantly improve efficiency, minimize stockouts, and optimize restocking schedules, allowing vending operators to save time and focus on scaling their business.

If you operate in multiple locations, cloud-based software can help you manage your entire fleet of machines from a single dashboard. You can track sales, monitor maintenance needs, and even adjust prices remotely, all from your computer or smartphone.

Most cloud-based software solutions integrate seamlessly with modern vending machines and are compatible with older machines after retrofitting. You can customize the software to send notifications for low stock, machine malfunctions, or maintenance needs. This reduces the number of unnecessary site visits and helps you stay proactive in addressing issues before they affect sales.

The software also gives you the ability to analyze sales trends and performance data. You can see which products sell best in specific locations, identify underperforming machines, and make data-driven decisions to improve profitability. With features like remote price adjustments, you can quickly respond to changes in demand or implement promotions across all your machines with just a few clicks.

Some popular cloud-based vending management software solutions include Parlevel, VendSoft, and Cantaloupe (formerly USA Technologies). These platforms offer comprehensive features such as real-time sales tracking, inventory management, and remote monitoring.

- ***Parlevel*** provides an intuitive dashboard to manage machine performance, track sales trends, and handle route optimization.
- ***VendSoft*** is known for its user-friendly interface and powerful analytics that help you monitor sales and restocking needs.
- ***Cantaloupe*** offers advanced features like cashless payment integration, remote management, and detailed reporting, making it ideal for larger vending operations. These tools help streamline operations and maximize profitability.

Embracing Change

While technology can make running a vending business easier, it's important to choose the tools that fit your specific needs. You don't have to invest in every new gadget or software that comes along. Start with what will have the biggest impact on your business and grow from there.

For me, the shift to cashless payments and remote monitoring was a no-brainer. It made my life easier and helped increase sales. But you might find that other technologies, like smart inventory systems or digital displays, are what will take your business to the next level.

To stay updated on new innovations and tech in the vending industry, it's essential to follow industry publications, join online vending communities, and attend trade shows or conferences like the National Automatic Merchandising Association (NAMA) events. Subscribing to newsletters from vending equipment manufacturers and tech providers can also keep you informed about the latest tools and trends. Additionally, keeping an eye on emerging payment solutions, smart machine features, and software updates will help you stay competitive and integrate cutting-edge technology into your business.

Technology is all about making your business run more efficiently and profitably. By staying open to new innovations and tools, you can continue to grow and adapt in an ever-changing industry.

Up next: we'll look at one of the most critical aspects of running a successful business: customer service. Whether it's handling complaints, responding to feedback, or building lasting relationships, how you manage customer interactions can make or break your vending business.

CHAPTER 13:
Customer Service Excellence

Customer service isn't just a component of a business—it is the heart of it. Whether you're running a retail shop, a real estate business, or managing a vending machine empire, the satisfaction of your customers directly impacts your success. No matter how advanced your technology or how efficient your processes are, neglecting customer service can derail even the most promising businesses.

At its core, customer service is about creating an experience where people feel valued, understood, and appreciated. When customers feel like their needs are heard, they are more likely to return and recommend your services to others. In the long run, great customer service is a strategy that pays off by building loyalty and encouraging repeat business. On the other hand, poor service can quickly lead to negative reviews, damaged relationships, and a drop in sales.

The Benefits of Exceptional Customer Service

The benefits of focusing on customer service extend far beyond just making a sale. Businesses with excellent customer service can expect:

- ***Increased customer retention:*** Customers who feel valued will come back again and again.
- ***Positive word-of-mouth referrals:*** Satisfied customers are your best marketing tool, recommending your business to friends and family.
- ***Stronger brand reputation:*** A solid track record of great service can distinguish your business in a crowded marketplace.
- ***Fewer complaints and disputes:*** Handling issues well minimizes conflicts and builds trust.

Now, let me tell you about a personal experience that really drove this home for me.

Years ago, in my real estate business, I had a situation that could have ended terribly. I was working with a client who had some very specific requirements for a property, and I thought I had found the perfect one. But I made an error during the negotiations—nothing intentional, just a misunderstanding that led to some big issues. The client was furious, and rightfully so. They were at the point of walking away, not just from this deal, but from doing business with my company altogether. It was a huge deal, both financially and reputationally, and I knew I had to take full responsibility.

Instead of getting defensive, I listened to the client's concerns. I stayed calm, never raising my voice, even though the client was livid. I apologized sincerely, took immediate action to correct the mistake, and kept them updated at every step of the process. It wasn't easy, but I managed to resolve the situation without any long-term damage to the transaction.

Months later, the same client came back for another deal. Surprised but grateful, I asked why they decided to continue working with me after that first incident. The client told me something I'll never forget: *"I was ready to walk away, but the way you handled the situation—your calm approach, how you took responsibility and fixed the issue—convinced me to give you another chance."*

That experience taught me that people don't just remember what you do when things are going well—they pay closer attention to how you act when something goes wrong. Since then, this client has referred me to multiple others, and we've done many successful deals together.

In the vending business, just like in real estate or any other industry, customer service is critical to long-term success. Whether you're interacting with the end customer who buys from your machine or the location manager who allows you to place your machines, how you handle these relationships can make or break your business.

For instance, a broken vending machine in a high-traffic area might seem like a minor inconvenience, but if not addressed quickly, it can damage your reputation. On the flip side, fixing the problem efficiently and showing that you care about customer experience can turn that situation around and even strengthen relationships.

Customer service is not just about avoiding problems; it's about actively engaging with customers, learning what they want, and building loyalty through trust and consistency.

The Importance of Customer Satisfaction

From the start of my vending machine business, I applied the lessons I had learned from real estate and other ventures: customer satisfaction is everything. One time, at a gym where I placed a vending machine, a customer mentioned that they liked the protein bars but were tired of the same flavors. I took this feedback seriously and swapped out the bars for some new options that aligned with their preferences. The result? Not only did my sales increase, but I also noticed more people using that machine regularly.

It's the small things, like listening and acting on feedback, that make all the difference. Customers want to feel heard, and when you show them that you're willing to make adjustments to meet their needs, they become more loyal. This loyalty translates into higher sales and long-term success.

Handling Complaints and Feedback

No matter how proactive you are, problems will happen. A machine might jam, a product might sell out too quickly, or a payment system might malfunction. When issues arise, how you handle complaints will determine whether you retain that customer or lose them forever.

I once had a vending machine in an office building that stopped accepting coins. Instead of waiting for complaints to pile up, I took action. I apologized to the building manager and rushed over to fix the machine. After I resolved the issue, I left a thank-you note for the customer who reported the problem. This small act of taking responsibility and resolving the issue quickly built trust and kept that machine's sales steady.

In customer service, the key is to stay calm, listen carefully, and show that you're taking steps to solve the problem. A quick, thoughtful response can turn a bad situation into a positive experience, which customers will remember.

Building Long-Term Relationships with Clients

In the vending business, long-term relationships with your clients—whether they are building managers, gym owners, or school administrators—are just as crucial as keeping the end customers happy. A solid relationship can lead to more business opportunities and even help you expand to new locations.

For example, I had a vending machine at a school that performed well for over a year. When the school wanted to add another machine, they could have easily gone with a competitor. But because I had built a strong relationship with the administration, they asked me to place the second machine as well. I had always been responsive, offered healthy options, and ran promotions for the school's events, which made them trust me more than other vendors.

Relationships built on trust, communication, and reliability can open doors that lead to growth and success.

Achieving Customer Service Excellence

If you're wondering how to provide excellent customer service in your vending business, here are some actionable steps:

- ***Listen to Feedback:*** Encourage customers to leave feedback about the products on your machines. Whether it's through notes, email, or social media, gathering input helps you make changes that matter.

- ***Respond Quickly:*** When an issue arises, act fast. Whether it's a broken machine or a product complaint, a quick response shows customers that you care.
- ***Build Relationships with Clients:*** Stay in regular contact with the businesses or locations where your machines are placed. Ask how things are going, and see if there's anything more you can do to meet their needs. This helps build trust and long-term partnerships.
- ***Make Small Changes:*** Sometimes, small adjustments, like switching out a product or offering a new flavor, can make a big difference in customer satisfaction.
- ***Go the Extra Mile:*** Whether it's leaving thank-you notes or offering discounts, showing appreciation goes a long way toward building loyalty.

By focusing on these areas, you'll not only improve customer satisfaction but also create a thriving, long-lasting business. Remember, the most successful businesses are those that prioritize people, not just profits.

CONCLUSION

As we come to the end of this book, I want to leave you with more than just business strategies and techniques. I want to leave you with a sense of confidence, a belief that no matter where you are on your journey, success is within your reach. The vending machine business, like any other venture, can be both challenging and deeply rewarding. If you've taken the advice I've shared and applied it thoughtfully, you are well on your way to building something truly special.

One of the most beautiful aspects of this business is how adaptable it is. While this book has focused on vending machines, the principles we've discussed—customer service, strategic planning, marketing, cash flow management, and persistence—are universal. You can take these core ideas and apply them to any business you want to start or improve, and you will see results.

I didn't write this book from a position of theory. Everything I've shared comes from my own experiences—both the successes and the mistakes. I've learned that when you treat your customers with respect, when you listen to feedback, and when you consistently strive to improve your business, you will not only make money, but you'll also build something meaningful and lasting.

That's the reward in all of this: creating a business that serves others while fulfilling your goals. It won't always be easy. There will be moments of doubt, of failure, and frustration. But those moments are part of the process, and they are what makes success taste so much sweeter when it finally comes. Every challenge you overcome brings you one step closer to the goals you've set.

I want you to know that you are capable of this. You've already shown commitment by reading this book, and now you have a solid foundation to build on. Don't be afraid to take the leap, to make mistakes, and to learn from them. Success is not about never failing; it's about failing, learning, and growing.

Above all, remember that this business, and any other business you pursue, is about the people. Whether it's your customers, your clients, or your team, building strong relationships and offering real value will always set you apart. If you stay true to that, the rewards will follow—not just in financial success, but in the satisfaction of knowing you've built something that matters.

So go out there and make it happen. You've got this.

APPENDICES

Appendix 1: Sample Business Plan for Vending Machine Business

Executive Summary

Our vending machine business, *[Your Company Name]*, aims to provide convenient and accessible snacks, beverages, and other everyday items in high-traffic locations. By focusing on cashless payment systems, remote monitoring, and a customer-first approach, we intend to grow our business steadily within the first three years of operation. The business will start with an initial placement of five vending machines in local office buildings and gyms, with plans to expand to schools and retail locations in the second year.

Business Overview

[Your Company Name] is a sole proprietorship established to serve both businesses and consumers by offering a range of products through automated vending machines. We plan to cater to health-conscious consumers by providing healthy snack options alongside traditional offerings. Our business will benefit from cashless payment systems and modern vending technology, ensuring a smooth and convenient customer experience.

Objectives

- ***First Year:*** Successfully place 5 machines in key locations and achieve monthly revenue of $1,000 per machine.
- ***Second Year:*** Expand to 15 machines across 10 additional locations.
- ***Third Year:*** Explore partnerships with schools and retail chains, increasing machine count to 30.
- Maintain a customer satisfaction rating of 90% or higher.

Market Research

The vending machine industry in the U.S. is experiencing steady growth, with cashless payment options and healthier snacks driving consumer demand. According to market studies, businesses offering diverse product selections and cashless convenience see a 30% increase in sales compared to cash-only operators. Locations such as office buildings, gyms, schools, and hospitals are high-traffic areas where vending machines consistently perform well.

Target Market

Our primary customers are professionals in office complexes, students in schools, and fitness enthusiasts at gyms. These groups typically seek convenient access to snacks, drinks, and meal replacements. We will tailor the products in each machine based on customer preferences in different locations, using data collected through remote monitoring.

Products and Services

We will offer a range of snacks, beverages, and health-conscious products like protein bars, low-sugar drinks, and gluten-free snacks. The product selection will be regularly updated based on customer feedback and sales data from our machines.

In addition to standard offerings, we plan to offer premium services such as advertising placements on our machines' digital screens for local businesses, further increasing revenue.

Competitive Advantage

Our business will stand out by:

- Offering cashless payment options.
- Using remote monitoring technology to optimize restocking and customer satisfaction.
- Emphasizing healthier snack choices tailored to specific locations.
- Building strong relationships with location owners and maintaining consistent communication.

Operations Plan

- ***Machine Procurement:*** Purchase or lease five state-of-the-art vending machines with cashless payment capabilities and remote monitoring.
- ***Location Acquisition:*** Secure contracts with local gyms, office buildings, and schools to place machines.
- ***Supplier Contracts:*** Partner with local snack providers, beverage suppliers, and health food brands.
- ***Daily Operations:*** Use remote monitoring to track stock levels and manage restocking and maintenance. Ensure machines are fully stocked with high-demand products at all times.
- ***Growth Strategy:*** Scale by reinvesting profits into purchasing more machines and entering new high-traffic locations.

Financial Plan

Startup Costs

- ***Vending Machines (5 machines at $3,000 each):*** $15,000
- ***Installation and Setup:*** $2,000
- ***Initial Product Inventory:*** $3,000
- ***Licensing and Permits:*** $1,000
- ***Marketing and Promotions:*** $1,000
- ***Total Startup Costs:*** $22,000

Revenue Projections

Year 1:

Average Monthly Sales per Machine: $1,000

Monthly Revenue (5 machines): $5,000

Annual Revenue: $60,000

Year 2:

Monthly Revenue (15 machines): $15,000

Annual Revenue: $180,000

Year 3:

Monthly Revenue (30 machines): $30,000

Annual Revenue: $360,000

Break-even Analysis

We expect to break even by the end of Year 2, with consistent revenue from established machines and additional revenue from expanding into new locations.

Conclusion

With a clear plan for growth, strategic placement of machines, and a focus on customer satisfaction, *[Your Company Name]* will become a leading vending machine operator in the region. By leveraging technology and maintaining strong relationships with location owners, we will create a sustainable and profitable business.

Appendix 2: Checklist for Starting Your Vending Machine Business

Starting a vending machine business involves multiple steps that go beyond just buying machines and stocking them. This comprehensive checklist will guide you through every crucial detail to set up and operate your vending business successfully.

1. Research and Planning

Determine Your Niche: Decide what kind of vending machines you want to operate (e.g., snacks, beverages, healthy foods, specialty items).

Conduct Market Research: Study your local area's demand for vending machines, location opportunities, and consumer preferences.

Evaluate Competition: Identify who your competitors are and how you can differentiate your business (e.g., through product selection or location strategy).

Understand Regulations: Research local regulations regarding vending machines, including health and safety requirements, business licenses, and zoning laws.

Set Business Goals: Establish short-term and long-term business goals, such as the number of machines you want to operate and revenue targets.

2. Financial Planning

Estimate Startup Costs: Calculate initial expenses, including machine purchases, inventory, licenses, insurance, and transportation.

Determine Operational Costs: Account for ongoing expenses like restocking, maintenance, electricity, transaction fees for cashless payments, and any commissions to location owners.

Create a Budget: Outline your financial plan, detailing expected revenue, costs, and profit margins.

Secure Funding: Decide how to finance your business (e.g., personal savings, small business loans, or investors).

Plan for Taxes: Ensure you understand local tax requirements and register for any necessary tax IDs.

3. Legal and Administrative Setup

Register Your Business: Choose a business structure (e.g., sole proprietorship, LLC) and register your vending machine business with the appropriate authorities.

Get Necessary Permits and Licenses: Apply for vending permits and health department approvals (if selling food), and check if any other local licenses are required.

Obtain Insurance: Get liability insurance for your machines to cover potential damages, theft, or legal claims.

Open a Business Bank Account: Keep your business finances separate by setting up a dedicated business account.

Set Up Accounting and Bookkeeping: Invest in accounting software or hire an accountant to manage your financial records.

4. Vending Machine Acquisition

Choose the Right Vending Machine Type: Decide whether to purchase or lease machines and determine which type best fits your product offering (e.g., snack, drink, combo machines).

New vs. Used Machines: Consider whether to buy new machines for reliability or used machines for cost savings. Be sure to inspect used machines thoroughly.

Choose a Supplier: Identify reputable vending machine suppliers and request quotes.

Select Features: Decide whether to invest in machines with additional features like cashless payments, energy efficiency, or remote monitoring systems.

Plan for Machine Placement: Measure potential locations to ensure machines will fit, and understand the logistics of installation.

5. Location Setup

Scout Locations: Find high-traffic areas with potential customers, such as gyms, schools, offices, hospitals, and apartment complexes.

Negotiate with Location Owners: Discuss terms for placing your vending machines (e.g., commissions or rental fees) and ensure agreements are in writing.

Get Contracts in Place: Formalize all agreements with location owners to outline terms, responsibilities, and duration of the placement.

Verify Power Sources: Ensure the location has access to electricity and any other requirements your machine might need.

6. Product Sourcing and Inventory

Select Products: Choose popular items based on your niche and customer preferences. You may want to offer a mix of healthy, indulgent, and specialty options.

Find Suppliers: Build relationships with local or wholesale suppliers for better pricing on products.

Test Products: Consider testing new items in select machines before rolling them out to all locations.

Inventory Management: Implement a system for tracking inventory levels and ensuring machines are always stocked with fresh products.

Seasonal Adjustments: Be ready to rotate products based on seasons or holidays (e.g., cold drinks in summer, hot beverages in winter).

7. Operations and Maintenance

Set a Maintenance Schedule: Plan regular machine maintenance to prevent breakdowns and keep machines running smoothly.

Install Cashless Payment Systems: Set up card readers and mobile payment options to cater to cashless consumers.

Monitor Sales: Use remote monitoring systems to track sales, identify issues, and know when to restock without physically visiting each machine.

Create a Route Plan: Plan efficient restocking routes to minimize fuel costs and time.

Keep Machines Clean: Regularly clean machines to ensure hygiene and maintain a professional appearance.

8. Customer Service

Set Up a Complaint System: Provide clear contact information for customers to report issues with your machines.

Respond Quickly to Complaints: Be proactive in addressing customer feedback or machine malfunctions to maintain a positive reputation.

Build Relationships with Location Managers: Regularly check in with your location partners to ensure satisfaction and explore additional placement opportunities.

9. Marketing and Promotion

Brand Your Business: Create a recognizable logo and brand identity that stands out in your machines and promotional materials.

Online Presence: Build a website or social media profiles to market your vending business, highlight your locations, and communicate with customers.

Run Promotions: Offer discounts, run contests, or highlight new products through your machines to encourage customer engagement.

Leverage Local Influencers: Partner with local influencers or micro-influencers to promote your vending machines in specific communities.

10. Review and Improve

Track Sales and Performance: Regularly analyze your machines' performance to identify trends, popular products, and low-performing items.

Collect Feedback: Ask for feedback from customers and location owners to see how you can improve your offerings and services.

Stay Informed: Keep up with trends and technological advancements in the vending industry to remain competitive and efficient.

About the Author

Lena Voss is an accomplished business leader, writer, and researcher with a wealth of experience across multiple industries, including the ever-evolving world of vending machines. With years of hands-on experience in sectors ranging from technology to retail, Lena has developed a unique perspective on what drives success in both traditional and emerging markets.

In this book, Lena shares the practical strategies that have helped her thrive in the vending machine business—a field where innovation and customer insight are key. From selecting the right equipment to securing prime locations and maximizing profits, her guidance is invaluable for entrepreneurs looking to break into this industry or expand their existing ventures.

Her career is rich with practical lessons and insights, from empowering independent thinking to integrating ESG (Environmental, Social, and Governance) principles. Lena is committed to helping entrepreneurs and leaders grow sustainable businesses that thrive through innovation.

Through her writing, Lena shares key strategies to navigate modern challenges, balance regulatory demands, and leverage new technologies. Her approach combines compelling storytelling with actionable advice, providing readers a practical roadmap to business growth and success

Reference

[i] *National Automatic Merchandising Association. (2023). Retrieved from* *https://namanow.org/*

[ii] *World Metrics. (2024). Vending Industry Statistics: Revenue Soars, Industry Evolution Projected Growth. Retrieved from* *https://worldmetrics.org/vending-industry-statistics/*

[iii] *Vending Locator. (2023). Vending Machine Statistics in 2023. Retrieved from* *https://www.vendinglocator.com/blog/vending-machine-statistics*

[iv] *World Metrics. (2024). Vending Industry Statistics: Revenue Soars, Industry Evolution Projected Growth. Retrieved from* *https://worldmetrics.org/vending-industry-statistics/*

[v] *Verified Market Research. (2024). Global Smart Vending Machines Market Size By Technology, By Application, By End-User Industry, By Geographic Scope And Forecast. Retrieved from* *https://www.verifiedmarketresearch.com/product/smart-vending-machines-market/*

[vi] *Frontiers in Nutrition. (2021). College Students' Perception of Snacks Sold in Vending Machines in the US: A Mixed-Methods Study. Retrieved from* *https://www.ncbi.nlm.nih.gov/pmc/articles/PMC8578334/*

[vii] *BMC Public Health. (2015). Students' perspectives on promoting healthful food choices from campus vending machines: a qualitative interview study. Retrieved from* *https://www.ncbi.nlm.nih.gov/pmc/articles/PMC4446908/*

[viii] *Current Developments in Nutrition. (2020). Snacking Practices and Diet Choices Among College Students at a Large University in South Florida: A Cross-Sectional Survey. Retrieved from* *https://www.ncbi.nlm.nih.gov/pmc/articles/PMC7257333/*

[ix] *Hartsfield-Jackson Atlanta International Airport. ATL Fact Sheet. Retrieved from* *https://www.atl.com/about-atl/atl-factsheet/*

[x] *American Public Transportation Association. (2020). Public Transportation Facts.*

. Retrieved from https://www.apta.com/news-publications/public-transportation-facts/

[xi] *American Hospital Association. (2024). Fast Facts on U.S. Hospitals, 2024. Retrieved from https://www.aha.org/statistics/fast-facts-us-hospitals*

[xii] *Data USA. (2023). Warehousing and storage sector report. Retrieved from https://datausa.io*

[xiii] *Statista. (2024). Monthly number of full-time employees in the United States from September 2022 to September 2024. Retrieved from https://www.statista.com/statistics/192361/unadjusted-monthly-number-of-full-time-employees-in-the-us/*

[xiv] *Multi Family Dive. (2022). Apartment statistics in the U.S.. Retrieved from https://www.multifamilydive.com*

[xv] *National Automobile Dealers Association. (2023). Franchised dealership statistics. Retrieved from https://www.nada.org*

[xvi] *American Hotel & Lodging Association. Hotel statistics in the U.S.. Retrieved from https://www.ahla.com/issue/travel-and-tourism*

[xvii] *International Health, Racquet & Sportsclub Association. (2020). The 2020 IHRSA Global Report. Retrieved from https://healthandfitness.org/publications/the-2020-ihrsa-global-report/*

[xviii] *Research.com. (2024). Number of Public Schools in the US: Key 2024 Data on States & Demographics. Retrieved from https://research.com/universities-colleges/number-of-public-schools-in-the-us*

[xix] *Statista. (2024). Undergraduate enrollment in U.S. universities 2011-2023. Retrieved from https://www.statista.com/statistics/235406/undergraduate-enrollment-in-us-universities/*

[xx] *National Retail Federation. (2021). Retail Sales to Now Exceed $4.44 Trillion in 2021, as NRF Revises Annual Forecast. Retrieved from https://nrf.com/media-center/press-releases/retail-sales-now-exceed-444-trillion-2021-nrf-revises-annual-forecast*

[xxi] *Fueleconomy.gov. Gas station statistics in the U.S.. Retrieved from https://www.fueleconomy.gov*

[xxii] *Worldmetrics.org. (2024). US Shopping Mall Statistics: Insights into Retail, Visitors, and Tenants. Retrieved from https://worldmetrics.org/us-shopping-mall-statistics/*

[xxiii] *Statista. (2024). City parks in with the highest visitation in the United States. Retrieved from https://www.statista.com/statistics/190057/number-of-visitors-to-city-parks-in-the-us-2009/*

[xxiv] *Carwash. (2022). Driving repeat carwash business. Retrieved from https://www.carwash.com/driving-repeat-carwash-business/*

[xxv] *Live Nation. (2019). Live Nation Entertainment Reports Fourth Quarter & Full Year 2019 Results. Retrieved from https://www.livenationentertainment.com/2020/02/live-nation-entertainment-reports-fourth-quarter-full-year-2019-results/*

[xxvi] *IBISWorld. (2023). Bars & Nightclubs in the US - Market Size, Industry Analysis, Trends and Forecasts (2024-2029). Retrieved from https://www.ibisworld.com/united-states/market-research-reports/bars-nightclubs-industry/*

[xxvii] *Pantone Color Institute. (2020). The Influence of Color on Brand Recognition. Retrieved From https://www.pantone.com/color-consulting/about-pantone-color-institute*

[xxviii] *Forbes. (2018). 10 Marketing, Web Design & Branding Statistics To Help You Prioritize Business Growth Initiatives. Retrieved From https://www.forbes.com/sites/gabrielshaoolian/2018/08/10/10-marketing-web-design-branding-statistics-to-help-you-prioritize-business-growth-initiatives/*

[xxix] *Sprout Social. (2021). Consumer trends report. Retrieved from https://sproutsocial.com*

[xxx] *Scrip. (2023). The Effectiveness of Compensation in Maintaining Employee Retention. Retrieved From* *https://www.scirp.org/journal/paperinformation?paperid=126223*

[xxxi] *Yahoo Finance. (2023). Blockbuster Had The Opportunity To Buy Netflix For $50 Million. Retrieved From* *https://finance.yahoo.com/news/blockbuster-had-opportunity-buy-netflix-185915158.html*

[xxxii] *Federal Reserve. (2022). The Federal Reserve Payments Study: 2022 Triennial Initial Data Release. Retrieved From* *https://www.federalreserve.gov/paymentsystems/fr-payments-study.htm*

[xxxiii] *Square Up. (2021). After One Year of COVID-19, New Square Data Reveals the Share of Cashless Businesses Has More Than Doubled. Retrieved From* *https://squareup.com/us/en/press/making-change-4*

[xxxiv] *Global Market Insights. (2023). Inventory Management Software Market Size. Retrieved From* *https://www.gminsights.com/industry-analysis/inventory-management-software-market*

Made in the USA
Monee, IL
04 November 2026

67383333R00134